Flying People

Flying People

bringing you safe flying, every day

by

Graham Perry

with illustrations by *figment*

kea publishing

First published in 2004 by
kea publishing
14 Flures Crescent
Erskine
Renfrewshire PA8 7DJ
Scotland

Copyright © Graham Perry, 2004

British Library Cataloguing in Publication Data

Perry, Graham
Flying People : bringing you safe flying, every day
1.Aviation ground crews – History 2.Flight crews – History 3.Aeronautics – Safety
measures – History 4.Airlines – History 5.Aerospace engineering
I.Title
387.7'3'09

ISBN 0951895869

Printed in Scotland by Iain M. Crosbie Printers, Beechfield Road,
Willowyard Industrial Estate, Beith, Ayrshire KA15 1LN

Contents

Acknowledgements

Every person named in this book has helped to create it and of course many thousands of other 'flying people' have done so too. Some of the latter's names I never knew and never could - their influence and inspiration have come from the time when their experiences and mistakes appeared through word of mouth or on a printed page, to be shared with fellow flying people everywhere, me included. I thank them all. The names that follow, then, are just the tip of a very large iceberg because they represent a worldwide community of flying people who are the soul of this book. I would like to thank first Brian Riddle, the librarian of the Royal Aeronautical Society, who has been a great source of knowledge and help. I am grateful to the Editor of *Flight International* for his kind permission to quote from the journal, the assembled volumes of which form a unique and detailed weekly record of aeronautical progress over nearly a century. From industry I must thank Stuart Smith, Managing Director of Dunlop Aircraft Tyres, and Ron Vice, company historian at Dunlop Aerospace, for their enthusiastic help. Likewise, I thank Andrew Kempton and Dave Gibbons at Rolls-Royce plc and Graham Hand at Irvin-GQ Ltd. In the government and scientific community my thanks go first to Tom Kerr CB, former Director of the Royal Aircraft Establishment at Farnborough and of the National Gas Turbine Establishment at Pyestock, and the author of the excellent *Always a Challenge*. Also to Roy Maxwell and Arthur Cardrick from RAE Structures Department and to many other colleagues there and in the MoD with whom I had the privilege of working, in a very modest capacity, some twenty-five years ago. To Michael Dobson who has chronicled the work of RAE Bedford so well in his book *Wings Over Thurleigh*. To friends and working contacts at the Air Accidents Investigation Branch at Farnborough: Geoffrey Wilkinson, a distinguished former Chief Inspector of Accidents; Ron Shimmons and Peter Sheppard on the current staff; and not forgetting Eric Newton and Gilbert Jamieson who taught me so much while helping me solve the apparently unsolvable many years ago. All of them convinced me, without a struggle, that it is far better to be on the investigative side of air accidents than on the creative one.

Thanks to Brian Lewis and to many friends in the air traffic control community, remembering especially the late Bill Woodruff who died suddenly shortly after providing much vital material for this book. I would like to thank Peter Tait, the Chief Executive of CHIRP at Farnborough and his colleague David Johnson for their help and advice with Chapter 17. I am grateful to many former Royal Air Force colleagues, but particularly to Group Captain David Green, Wing Commander Peter Austin, Wing Commander Norman Want and Squadron Leader Ian Fairhead for their help with specific old memories. And from the airlines I must thank Brian Thorne and Captains Mike Clews, John McCormick and Mike Phillips for their input and inspiration. Of course, the word 'inspiration' hardly does justice to the contributions of Captain John Reed, *figment*, whose humour and genius produced the wonderful cartoons in this book.

My special thanks go to Iain Hutchison and his team at *kea publishing* for publishing this book, and I am grateful to many other flying people, colleagues and friends, who have contributed to these pages. Many will doubtless be relieved, after reading what follows, to have remained anonymous. I thank them all for their wit, wisdom and support. The book might not have been written at all without one friend in particular, who listened to the idea and said: "Go for it!" Having 'gone for it', any errors in the book - be they of recall, fact, spelling, grammar, punctuation or style - are mine. And all the views I have expressed are, of course, entirely my own.

Graham Perry

The publisher would like to express appreciation to David Doak and Douglas Nicolson for their assistance.

The inaugural meeting of the 'Man Will Never Fly' Memorial Society

1

"Man Will Never Fly"

In December 2003, man had allegedly been flying powered aircraft for one hundred years. I say 'allegedly' because it depends on whether or not you believe Wilbur and Orville Wright's publicity agent. OK, I will concede the photograph. But there was only one, and it was a very grainy affair. And in black and white! That could have been easily faked, surely? Significantly there was not a video camera or TV crew in sight. Personally, many of us regard it all as highly suspicious and find it very difficult to believe. No less a person than the editor of the *Dayton Daily News* said in early December 1903: "Man will never fly. And, if he does, he will not come from Dayton, Ohio." It should not surprise you then to learn that, in the USA, 'The Man Will Never Fly Memorial Society' exists and thrives to this day. It has branches all over the country which meet every year on the same day, 16 December, the eve of the anniversary of that (alleged) first flight. At every meeting the agenda is the same: members get positively pie-eyed at the unending scandal of yet another monstrous year of deception perpetrated on a gullible public. You don't believe me? If you use the internet, see the website 'www.manwillneverfly.com'. The Society's members believe that two Wrights made a wrong at Kitty Hawk in 1903. They believe that air travel is in fact a huge confidence trick, with people actually boarding not aircraft but Greyhound buses with wings. Whilst aboard these winged buses, passengers are given the illusion of flight as cloud-like scenery is moved past their windows in an expensive theatrical performance. Curiously, almost all the Society's members work in the aerospace business, many in very senior positions. One of the strongest memberships is centred on the aeronautical research laboratories at the USAF's Wright-Patterson Air Force Base near Dayton, Ohio. They should know.

This is a book about the last fifty years of aviation and, most importantly, about its people. Its very existence, therefore, rests on the uncomfortable assertion that Wilbur and Orville's publicity person was telling the absolute truth on that day in December 1903 and that man can actually fly. If those with experience of the political spin and commercial hype of the 20th and early 21st centuries can possibly accept that, and I agree it is a lot to ask, we are in business with this book. In business for what? Is this a history? Not really, but the brave reader reaching the end might feel some sense of the history of the last fifty years of aviation. Is it an autobiography? A bit here and there it may be but only, I hope, when a personal experience was one that was shared with very many others who have subsequently made their careers in aviation. Is it a technical book? Hardly, but there are some simple technical explanations to enable the reader to understand the stories told. If it is some of these things it is others too, and all together they are intended to add up to something else. The book is simply a slightly wry look at the past fifty years of flying, observed by someone who has been privileged to be involved with aviation and its people throughout much of that time. It celebrates the spirit of flying people by examining how they work, and by taking an affectionate look at the doings of just a few of the less well-known souls who have shaped aviation, and made it happen, over the past fifty years. Its purpose can be summed up no better than by paraphrasing the words of a former 1970s leader of the RAF Red Arrows aerobatic team, Squadron Leader Ian Dick, when he was talking about his team's display sequence: "...it is intended to amuse the knowledgeable, inform the interested, and scare nobody."

Histories of early aviation tend to be large coffee table books, full of pictures (of varying quality) featuring ancient pieces of very questionable engineering. In early photographs of military aviation, the flying machine always faces nose-to-camera which makes it very difficult to identify. Moreover, it is usually further hidden by a crowd of uniformed men whose garb invariably includes carefully wound puttees. A large English Sheepdog usually completes the sepia-toned picture. In contrast, early photographs of civil aircraft are quite different. In those, the ancient piece of aeronautical engineering in question usually serves in the picture as a large sideways backdrop to the principal human subject in the foreground, who is some establishment figure. This poor soul, whether male or female, is always wearing a hat and a rather tense smile, and appears to be pausing for a last photograph at the foot of the steps while plucking up the courage to defy both gravity and their mother's warning about "going up in one of those things".

Then, as aviation moved on from those early days of military and civil flying, the pictures changed too. Books about the later periods have more pictures of the air-to-air variety, where the people have somehow become incidental to the aircraft. The aircrew in those photographs are largely unseen, shadowy figures, wearing leather helmets and hidden behind very small windscreens or inside dark cockpits. Passengers too are generally unseen, perhaps just a glimpse of a hand at some window. The aircraft is the proud subject of the photograph, each bigger than the one before, more struts, more wires, more engines. Put together, however, all these pictures catalogue the nuts and bolts of aeronautical progress as the aviation community got bolder and wiser in the first fifty years of building and operating aircraft.

Bolder and wiser are the key words because it was usually in that order and at some cost. In the first fifty years of powered flight there was a lot of boldness, often not enough wisdom except in rueful hindsight, and the cost was high. The rate of technical progress was staggering however, leading as it did from the wood and canvas creations of 1903 to the jet air travel and supersonic flight of 1953. Doubtless, two world wars helped catalyse that rapid progress. But in the 1950s aircraft were still getting airborne with controls connected the wrong way round, or with one-way fuel valves fitted back to front, as a large number of smoking holes in the ground testified. A sift through the daily newspapers or weekly aviation magazines of that time reveals a quite frightening accident rate. Small wonder that the technical developments of the past fifty years have necessarily been a little less bold, and instead have been about making things safer, more reliable and generally better. During those years aviation's people have

10

concentrated on gaining, consolidating and circulating the wisdom of the aviation profession. That very difficult and sometimes painful process has involved the intellect, initiative and cooperation of everybody involved with aircraft, whatever their role.

In many modern organisations knowledge is kept and deliberately not shared because, in the culture of those organisations, 'knowledge is power'. You can recognise these places; perhaps you even work in one. They are where the support staff achieve almost all their job satisfaction from seeing how long it takes for senior managers to find out what they and the other junior staff already know. The aviation community tends not to be like that. With aircraft builders and operators, knowledge has become a commodity to be shared as quickly as possible, in the hope that by being shared it will prevent someone paying the cost of discovering it the hard way all over again. That cost could after all, as it has done many times in the past, involve losing lives. Aviation's people think this way in their technical work, and this same philosophy tends to spill over into the way they relate to other people. Flying people are communicative, open and fun. They are the reason why working with aircraft is so satisfying and enjoyable.

So this may be a book about aircraft and flying, but its theme is the inspiration and character of the thousands of people that have made (and continue to make) it all possible. Very many of them came into the aviation profession because an early interest in aeroplanes brought them into contact with aircraft and flying people through the Air Cadets, as described in the next few chapters, and they found those experiences to be a life-changing revelation. Only a handful of those men and women, some identified but many still working and resolutely un-named ("I'll stay anonymous, thank you very much!"), can find their way into a book of this size. As some of the tales unfold the reader will enjoy imagining the nature of the characters involved. Cheerful cynicism abounds in aviation's people. Their conscientiousness or resolve, however, will need no imagination because those and other personal qualities will be readily apparent. The few individuals who have found their way into these pages represent a huge community of dedicated aviation people who, especially in the second half-century of flight, have made it their life's work to make air travel so commonplace, safe and affordable.

For those readers for whom flying and aircraft are mysteries, especially for those for whom they are frightening mysteries, I hope this book will help de-mystify things and reassure you. Aviation's people are the key to your understanding and peace of mind. Understand their spirit, and how they work and think, and you will begin also to understand and appreciate why you are safe in their hands and why aircraft work as they do. And starting to understand the spirit of flying people is really very simple: on 16 December each year, the anniversary of the eve of that alleged first powered flight in 1903, raise a glass with me and countless others in the aircraft business and toast, if you will, 'The Man Will Never Fly Memorial Society'.

2

Fifties Inspiration

Fifty years ago, what attracted the young people of that time into aviation? For the first time in years it wasn't coercion by the military. The Second World War was history, something their fathers had been involved in and wouldn't talk about. And it wasn't National Service, which was being thankfully phased out. Yet thousands of youngsters, from a very early age, resolved that absolutely nothing other than working on, near, or in some way associated with aircraft would satisfy them for a career. Fifty years later they have become the generation who can be seen as the consolidators, building on the early post-war work of the wartime operators. It is they who have had the task, during their working lives, of making flying more commonplace, safer, cheaper and quieter.

To be a youngster in the 1950s needs some scene-setting. Life in Britain in the early 1950s was, for all but those with family money, characterised by what we would judge today to be domestic poverty. If your family was lucky, such poverty seemed to be slowly declining, but for most people the early post war years were hard. Ration Books seemed to dominate family life in 1950, together with shops with thinly stocked shelves. Food was scarce and of uneven quality. Margarine and cooking fat came as big blocks to be cut into ounce chunks in grocers' shops and sold for cash plus ration coupons. The egg ration for an adult was one per week, and about one egg in four was bad so you cracked each one in a cup before committing it to the frying pan. There were no supermarkets because there was little available to put in them, and anyway the concept that you could put anything in your basket that hadn't already been paid for was absolutely ludicrous. Central heating did not exist, which was just as well because refrigerators were what they had in America and you needed a cold house to prevent the food going 'off'. The kitchen boiler went out most nights even if you had coal ration left and you could afford the coal; if you couldn't or the coal people couldn't deliver it, the boiler stayed out and you stayed cold. All household money went on essentials, food and fuel; there was little left over for anything else. Children were made to drink Government-issue 'orange juice', a description that from 1968 would surely constitute a case for the Trade Descriptions Act. This came in concentrated form, in little bottles with blue screw tops, and presumably contained just enough vitamin C to fend off scurvy. As if this wasn't enough, children also got two spoonfuls per day of Government Cod Liver Oil. There could be no challenge under the Trade Descriptions Act for this one, as it tasted exactly as the label suggested. The Human Rights Act possibly would have been nearer the mark. Rumour had it that Cod Liver Oil would prevent rickets, and a whole generation of early post-war youngsters remain unconvinced to this day that rickets were the greater evil as they were cruelly denied the opportunity to try those instead.

Each of Britain's major cities seemed to be one big bombsite. Going to London, for example, on the train from Kent was to witness a rising devastation as the train passed Lewisham and New Cross and approached London Bridge. With the merchant ships of the Empire unloading at the docks in the distance, the houses at the side of the track revealed a succession of great holes in rows of buildings, with rotting curtains and peeled wallpaper flapping in the breeze, and baths hanging crazily out of walls, thirty feet up. But, to a youngster, life was life with nothing better to compare it with or get envious about so it was not sad, just interesting. And it was very apparent that many other interesting and incredible things were happening in the world outside one's own immediate, subsisting life.

One man remembers being a four-year old with his grandfather in a small park in Camberwell, London, one afternoon when a Comet airliner flew over. His grandfather died in December 1949 so in the summer of that year this must have been the first prototype, perhaps on its first ever flight from Hatfield over London into London Airport (later Heathrow). The approaching scream of the engines was the first thing to grab their attention, then they both got up from the park bench to try to see what was making the noise as this dark shape appeared directly overhead through the full-leafed plane trees. The sight of it was unforgettable, directly overhead and low, "all silvery" (to a four-year-old) with smooth, curved lines under the inner wings where the jets were housed. Then, just as suddenly, with a roar replacing the screaming, it was gone. He says that the comparison between that brief sight and the surroundings that remained – the still bombed-out ruins of St Giles Hospital – was dramatic. He didn't know what it was. His grandfather didn't know what it was. But it didn't scare him, it was magic. How could anybody not want to fly in that? Or, if you couldn't fly in it, to see it up close, touch it, smell it? At the age of four, after brief flirtations with buses and trains (to which he will admit only if pressed), the lad was hooked. On aeroplanes.

But whether you were fascinated by aeroplanes or not, by 1951 it was clear to any young person from all the talk about the Festival of Britain that many new developments and technologies were afoot, and that there was something for everyone. Architecture, for a start. The temporary Skylon and the Dome of Discovery on the South Bank exhibition site. The inspiring Royal Festival Hall, still inspiring to this day with its huge concert hall suspended like a giant Easter egg in a basket. And engineering. Nuclear power stations. New trains, new buses, new ships, new vehicles for exploring Antarctica (SnoCats), new everything. Each week, Marcus Morris' excellent *Eagle* comic featured in its centre pages a cut-away diagram of something technological and new. Those diagrams were fascinating for anyone who was interested in new technology, and an education in itself for a budding engineer or scientist. Just how good they were is borne out by the story of what happened to L. Ashwell Wood, who drew the diagram of the English Electric P.1B, the prototype destined to be the RAF's new fighter and yet to be called the Lightning. The morning that edition of *Eagle* was published, Mr Wood was arrested under the Official Secrets Act and questioned about how he knew about the detailed internal layout of the aircraft, especially the engine installation. It took him some time to convince the authorities that he didn't know – he had worked it out. And, being a technical illustrator and an engineer, he had worked it out exactly right. Presumably the nice people in technical intelligence in the Warsaw Pact had worked it out as well, but Mr Wood's arrest must have told them what the correct answer was, even if they had got it wrong. One teenage schoolboy cut out and kept the P.1B Lightning diagram, along with many others, and was pleased that he did so because it came in useful. Twenty-five years later it hung on his office wall at RAF Binbrook in Lincolnshire where somehow he had been entrusted with the engineering of seventy Lightnings, the whole RAF force by that time.

To be air-minded in the 1950s was to be in a sort of aeronautical heaven. The Canberra bomber that Roland Beamont flew like a fighter at air displays with a twinkle in his eye. Sonic bangs at the Farnborough Air Show, where the local glaziers prospered in the 1950s like the local caterers do now. The Viscount airliner, the world's first to be powered by a propeller turbine, in which it was said that you could stand a coin on its edge on the tables between the seats and the aircraft's motion was so smooth that the coin wouldn't fall over. The Brabazon, Bristol's aluminium overcast, in the solid hands of Bill Pegg. The V-bombers, the Valiant, Vulcan and Victor, painted all white to reflect the flash of a nuclear weapon if ever they were called upon to deliver one, having failed in their mission of deterrence. Roly Falk actually rolling the Vulcan at an air display, defying both Avro's management and, seemingly, the laws of physics with such a big aircraft. Neville Duke's world air speed record in the Hawker Hunter off Littlehampton, Mike Lithgow's in the Supermarine Swift a few days later, then Peter Twiss's in the Fairey Delta 2, a stunning 1,132 mph. As well as the successes to enjoy, however, there were the tragedies to understand: the early Comets and their shocking unexplained losses; the de Havilland 110 breaking up over Farnborough in 1952 when the wing failed at high speed; a Vulcan suffering the same fate a few years later as it rolled and pulled out of a high speed dive at a Battle of Britain display at RAF Syerston. Certainly, to be air-minded in the 1950s was to be excited by aviation's possibilities, but that excitement was definitely tempered by a realisation that flying could be inherently dangerous. What an opportunity, to make it less so! That turned out to be the definitive challenge of the second fifty years of flight, to make it as safe as possible. More efficient, yes; more affordable, yes; quieter, yes; and other things too. But safer, above all else, even for military aircraft because they were becoming more and more expensive. Cut an aircraft operator or designer in half to see what he or she is made of and, any decent pathologist will tell you, it is safety that oozes out.

As a child in the early 1950s it was not easy to indulge a passion for aeroplanes. Few had access to a family car and not everyone was lucky enough to live near an interesting airfield. But there were models to build. Messrs E. Keil & Co of Wickford, Essex, sold a range of *KeilKraft* aircraft kits consisting of thin marked-out sheets of balsa wood and tissue. Hours of painstaking work with a sharp knife, balsa cement, tissue paste and dope resulted in, if you had been sufficiently patient, something flyable. Starting with gliders, moving up through rubber-powered single propeller types, the real enthusiasts bought little diesel engines (the E. D. 'Bee') and built fast control-line models, free-flight aircraft ('free-flight' being a euphemism for 'I lost it the second time I flew it') and even radio-controlled models. Aero-modelling could also provide an early experience of the realities of aerodynamics and engineering. Strapping your new model proudly to the carrier of your bike and cycling off at speed down to the park for its first flight, you discovered quickly what happens when wings are forced through the air at a large angle to the airflow: they fail upwards with a sharp crack and clap hands above the fuselage. Back to the balsa cement, tissue and dope. But models weren't the real thing and somehow the sharp nylon propellers (and the diesel fuel getting into the cuts they made) inflicted more pain and injury than a real aircraft seemingly ever could. If real aircraft were your passion, the local cinema offered some black and white satisfactions (*Reach for the Sky, The Dam Busters*), but the best rewards came from keeping one's wits about you and looking up. Our house in north Kent was on the extended centreline of Biggin Hill's runway 21, so pairs of recovering Royal Auxiliary Air Force weekend Meteors (and later, Hunters of No. 41 Squadron RAF) were the staple fare. In September, Battle of Britain displays at Biggin Hill produced flypasts of Lincolns, B-29s, Shackletons and Neptunes over the house. Plus the occasional exciting prototype (a Victor at low level, going back to Radlett around the east of London). Good eyesight and a clear day revealed the USAF's contribution to European security, condensation-trailing high from their bases in the Midlands and East Anglia: Boeing B-47 Stratojets, Convair B-36 bombers, Douglas B-66 Destroyers. And sometimes an RAF Valiant from Gaydon or Marham, all at 40,000 feet. Of the airliners, BEA's Douglas DC-3 'Pionair' class were most evident, flying eastwards over north Kent at about 3,000 feet en route to Brussels and beyond. BEA was 'British European Airways'; it said so on the side of their aircraft. But every schoolboy knew that it really stood for Back Every Afternoon.

Up close to real aircraft was the problem. Touching and smelling. Our annual holiday to Broadstairs (British Railways, luggage sent in advance) revealed, in addition to Manston's USAF F-86 Sabres and F-84 Thunderstreaks at low level over the sea, a little piston-engined aeroplane pottering clockwise around the Isle of Thanet all day long. A short bus ride and a long walk one afternoon took us to Ramsgate Airport, newly rebuilt and re-opened in 1953 after having been bombed during the war, and its collection of aircraft. It had two Tiger Moths for training, and the little pottering aeroplane giving the joy-rides was a Miles Messenger. Half an hour, nose pressed up against the fence and gate ('Only Passengers Past This Point') as it came and went, watching, listening, smelling. Ecstasy.

Ecstasy soon turned to shock. I was being asked if I would like to go for a trip. Unbelievable, as it was five whole shillings (25p), nearly six month's pocket money.

"Are you coming too?"

"No, I can't afford that, but I'd like you to go if you want to".

And so at the age of eight, on 4 August 1953, I got my feet off the ground for the first time. A middle-aged couple came too, the man sitting in the front starboard seat next to the pilot, the lady with me in the back. Up close the aircraft was bigger than it looked from a distance and the wing was high off the ground. I had to be lifted up over the huge flap on to the wing root so I could climb into the back seat. The first real surprise was the noise level of the engine when it started, but this and the bumpy taxi over the sun-baked grass to the runway were a good acclimatisation to the real noise and bumps as

Touching and smelling...

the aircraft started its take-off run. After just a few seconds the tail was up and you could see forwards and sideways as the aeroplane accelerated across the airfield in a flying attitude. In no time at all it was airborne, and I waved at the small figure of my father, standing trapped behind the corral of that fence. Then another surprise as the aircraft banked sharply to the right to avoid Manston's airspace and headed north-west towards Westgate.

I could not believe the fascinating beauty of the ground from the air. It was all so logical, the fact that buildings could be seen, cars could be just made out, but people hardly at all except as a texture on the beaches. The green of the countryside, the white of the surf and the blues and greens of the sea all seemed so much more pronounced from the air. The speed with which things slipped by was another revelation. Westgate, Margate, Kingsgate Bay, the North Foreland lighthouse with its queue of visitors leading up the path to its front door, then Broadstairs and a descent over Ramsgate back into the airfield, all in little more time than it takes to tell. The smooth descent and arrival at the runway's end, the nose raising gently, the engine reducing to just a tick-over and then the gentle rumble as the aircraft's wheels met the grass again. Thanet, all of it, in ten minutes from 600 feet and a lifetime memory; every cell in that little brain lapping up every second and storing it away for ever. Re-living the experience fifty years later by flying a light aircraft around Thanet releases the detail of all those memories because the summer colours are the same from the air. The only difference now is that this time you have to land on Manston's huge concrete runway and have your tea at the excellent flying school founded by the late Ted Girdler. Ramsgate Airport closed some forty years ago and pre-fabricated industrial buildings and houses now occupy the former big patch of green by the water tower.

Walking back into Broadstairs after that first flight my feet were still off the ground because I had a clear inch of air under each one. I am sure I bored for Britain at tea time, as only an entranced eight year-old can. I gathered that my mother had no idea that my father had any intention of sending me up on my own and it turned out that he didn't either. He just got so fed up with his eight-year-old's aeronautical one-track mind that he saw five shillings as a worthwhile investment to put him off aircraft for good, if that was the way it was to be. It wasn't.

That first flight set the pattern for a number of years, as it did for countless other youngsters hooked by the wonder of flight. Talk to any group of aviation types now in their late fifties and it's the same story, the annual flight at the seaside or, for the lucky ones, an occasional flight at a local airfield as a reward for washing aeroplanes or helping in some way. Just the locations are different: "an Auster on the beach at Cleethorpes" says one, "the Dragon Rapide on the Isle of Wight." say two more, "Blackpool, round the Tower!" says another. All year many of us would save our weekly pocket money, six months or more of which would be spent during our summer holiday on just ten more precious minutes airborne. More fun than sweets, and better for your teeth. All these flights were magical experiences and all were different. It was the differences that intrigued us then, as they do to this day. It is the differences that provide the challenge in every flight.

3

Flight for Beginners

Clearly there can never be any future in spending half a year's income on one passion, however important it may be (or however pretty she is). In the 1950s the clearest prospect of some free and interesting flying for young people came, as it does now, from one source: the Air Cadets. Some schools and most towns have a Combined Cadet Force (CCF) or Air Training Corps (ATC) squadron run by volunteer officers, NCOs and civilian instructors. In return for Friday nights during term time spent learning drill and studying airmanship, navigation, meteorology and the like, the cadet can look forward to some flying during the year with the Air Experience Flights dotted around the country, and at the annual summer camp on an RAF station. The newly joined cadet who is keen to fly can see it very much in this light, of effort leading to reward. Only later, with some flying experience under his or her belt, does the cadet begin to appreciate the whole offering and realise the immense personal benefits to be gained from learning the technical subjects associated with flight, from learning how to lead (and, just as important, how to be led), and from the experience of organising things for the benefit of others.

The Air Cadets provide an early demonstration of life's lessons and the benefits of some surprisingly unfashionable things. Top of this list is discipline. All aircraft bite fools. Anyone who approaches an aircraft casually, without alertness or thought, is riding for a very large fall. The Royal Air Force, as the world's oldest air force, should know. It has learned everything the hard way and, on the few occasions when it has dropped its guard and stopped remembering, it has learned things the hard way all over again. Consequently the seriousness of flying as a business is one of the longest lasting impressions an air cadet will take into later life. Everyone connected with the Service, from the most recently joined cadet to the most senior officer, reads the Defence Aviation Safety Centre's flight safety magazine *Aviate* (internal MoD Journal) and other material circulated on the subject. *Aviate* is the successor to the longest-lived of all flight safety magazines, the RAF's *Air Clues*, edited for forty-five years by the ever-alert (but now retired) 'Wing Commander Spry'. The magazines publicise the details of accidents and incidents, and comment on the lessons learned from them so that people do not make the same mistakes again. Even the most junior cadet will tell you that the three most important things in aviation are: safety, safety and safety. Safety comes from discipline. It is a disciplined line of cadets who do as they have been told, running in line with heads ducked directly towards the door of a rotors-turning Puma helicopter, once they are summoned to do so by a crewman. The stakes are too high to do otherwise. People in the past have tried it in more individual ways, many only once.

The aircraft that cadets of my generation got to know best for air experience flying was the Chipmunk. For years it was the RAF's basic trainer, designed by de Havilland

Canada in the late 1940s, an all-metal, aerobatic aircraft that is a challenge to fly well. It seats two, one behind the other, and so the pilot would sit in the front and the cadet, briefed to the eyeballs on what to expect when things went right and especially on what to do if things went wrong, would sit behind him. Some cadets were very small. On one squadron, a cadet was so small that even sitting on his parachute he couldn't see over the sides of the cockpit and out of the canopy. Undaunted, he still went flying and his friends eagerly awaited his return.

"Did you like it?"

"Yes, it was smashing!"

"What did you see?"

"Nothing."

RAF pilots seemed to enjoy flying cadets in Chipmunks. It was very common to be strapped into the rear seat with the engine running and, gathering your wits, to look toward the front cockpit to discover from the four rings on each shoulder that a Group Captain was flying you. In summer the Air Experience Flights (AEFs) would allocate their aircraft to the various RAF stations hosting cadet camps and there would be no shortage of station pilots volunteering to fly them. For some this could pose more of a challenge than they expected. RAF fast-jet pilots from the 1960s were trained from the start on the Jet Provost, then on the Folland Gnat and Hawker Hunter before converting on to their operational type. Unless they had been awarded a flying scholarship at school or had been on a University Air Squadron (UAS), few had ever flown anything with a propeller, let alone with a piston engine or a tail-wheel undercarriage. To some jet pilots it came as a rude shock to discover that you cannot land a light tail-wheel aircraft by flying it down the approach towards the runway numbers at high speed, flaring the attitude ever so slightly in the final seconds to thump it down, then streaming the brake parachute and relying on Messrs Irvin-GQ (brake chutes) and Dunlop (wheel brakes) to stop you in a straight line well before the other end of the runway. Light aircraft don't land like that. Try it and, if the speed is even a little too high when you flare, the aircraft will balloon upwards again and everyone, just everyone, in the crew-room and the control tower will notice. And, as for opening the throttle quickly and going around for another try, if the rudder pedals aren't moved exactly in sympathy as engine power increases, the aircraft will roll and turn as well. At low speed that can be dangerous. The jet pilot discovers the finesse of using the rudder for the first time as he tries to counter the effect of the spiral wake from the propeller that seems intent on messing up his flying. Jet aircraft go where you point them, but propeller-driven ones don't and more than one fast-jet pilot had some difficulty converting to the Chipmunk. What would the cadets have thought had they realised that their hero in the front was, in fact, a very chastened aviator who had scared himself (not to mention his Wing Commander Flying, seated in the back) several times just days before? They need not have worried; a chastened aviator is the best kind. Remember, all aircraft bite fools, and no one is more foolish than a complacent aviator.

As flying experience progresses, the air minded young person's attention wanders away from the novelties of things far below, and on to the various bits that make up the aircraft and cause it to fly in the way it does. There cannot be an aircraft passenger who has not looked out along the wing and wondered how on earth (shouldn't that be 'off-earth'?) it works. Some, doubtless, will turn their attention back to their in-flight entertainment system and prefer not to think about it, but for the interested here it is in the rest of this chapter, in a nutshell. 'How aircraft fly' in a few words and just three diagrams, the subject that RAF student pilots through the years have always called 'arrows'. See if you can work out why.

As an aircraft travels through the air it experiences drag from the airflow in the same way that your cupped hand experiences drag when you cautiously push it through an open car sunroof. To overcome that drag you need a pull or thrust, and that is provided by the propeller in a piston-engined aircraft or by the exhaust in a jet. If Thrust equals Drag, the aircraft will not accelerate or decelerate (as predicted by Sir Isaac Newton) and it will continue at the speed at which it is travelling. Those are the horizontal, forwards and backwards forces of flight and they balance out. Now we need to consider the vertical ones.

The aircraft has weight. Without a force to counter that weight it would accelerate towards the ground. But then, if you think about it, without some upwards force it would never have got off the ground in the first place so there cannot be anything to worry about in a flying aeroplane. The force that keeps it up is called Lift and, if Lift can be made to equal Weight, all will be well in the vertical direction too. The Lift is provided by the wing, which produces it from the airflow, the speed of the aircraft as it travels through the air. Just how it does that I will describe in a moment.

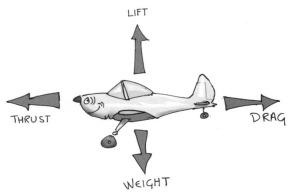

So we have four forces on our aircraft: Thrust and Drag horizontally, and Lift and Weight vertically. Ask yourself: what would happen if the engine power failed? Would the aircraft fall out of the sky? No, but the Drag would no longer be balanced by the Thrust, so the aircraft would slow down. Putting the nose down slightly and losing height gently would restore the speed and the aircraft would then be gliding downwards. In a glide with no thrust there are three forces instead of four. They are no longer at right angles, but they still balance each other out. The aircraft is not going to fall out of the sky.

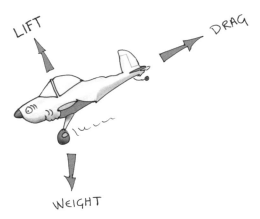

LIFT

DRAG

WEIGHT

All aeroplanes can glide. A high performance sailplane glides all the time once it has been launched and descends about one foot for every forty-five feet it travels forwards. From three thousand feet it could travel twenty-five miles in still air before landing. A jumbo jet in a powerless glide (yes, it has happened, and with an entirely happy outcome) will travel at least seventy-five miles from thirty-five thousand feet. An angry householder called a local flying club and demanded to know "what would happen if one of them aeroplanes has an engine stop right over my house?" The duty instructor had to tell him very gently that, in that unlikely eventuality, his house right underneath was exactly the safest place on earth to be. The householder was greatly reassured. So in future, when you read a newspaper or hear a TV report that goes 'the engine stopped and the aircraft fell to earth', you will know that this is absolute nonsense.

The clever bit about flying is the Lift developed by the wing from the airflow over its surfaces. It comes about from a simple physical principle. Any fistful of air encountered by the wing has two important properties for flying: it has a pressure, and it has speed. The French physicist Bernoulli discovered that these two properties were linked because added together they came to a constant value. So we can swap one for the other. 'Pressure plus speed equals a constant' means that if we can slow down a parcel of air we get a higher pressure. If we can speed it up, we get a lower pressure. This is what the wing takes advantage of. A wing is very curved on top and flatter underneath. Air travelling over the top surface speeds up slightly as it races to travel over the curve and its pressure goes down. That sucks the wing upwards. Air travelling underneath the wing slows down slightly and its pressure rises. That pushes up on the wing. The suction on the top surface and the push on the underside give you the Lift you need to balance your weight, and to fly.

It should be that easy: Lift counters the Weight, Thrust counters the Drag. Four forces in exact equality and opposition, and all an aircraft should therefore consist of is a tube (called a fuselage) to house the pilots and passengers, some engines to provide the thrust and a wing to provide the lift. A moment's thought, however, shows that it is not possible to do it this easily. To balance vertically for example, the total lift would have to act upwards along exactly the same line as the weight acted downwards. Even if you managed to load the aircraft so this was achieved, all a pilot would have to do would be to lean forward in the cockpit to operate a switch and the centre of gravity of the aircraft would move forwards, pitching the aircraft nose down. Not really practical for the pilot, to say nothing of the passengers who might object to being restrained in straitjackets for the entire duration of the flight. In reality, things are arranged so that the lift acts upwards slightly behind the line in which the weight acts downwards.

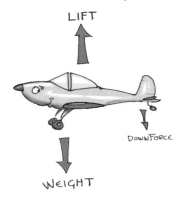

To prevent the aircraft pitching nose down as a result, another horizontal flying surface, called the tail, is introduced at the rear of the aircraft to produce a small downwards force in level flight. This downwards force can be adjusted, or trimmed, to cope with the exact weight and lift being experienced by the aircraft at any time. This is a constant process because fuel gets used up during flight and of course people like to move around. Another advantage of this arrangement, with a small down load on the tail, is that if the aircraft slows down slightly, causing the tail download to reduce as the airflow decreases, the effect of the aircraft's weight is to point the nose of the aircraft gently downwards so that it re-gathers speed and lift, and balance is restored. If the aircraft speeds up, the extra downwards force on the tail raises the nose and the aircraft slows down again as it climbs. The aircraft is then said to be stable in that it will recover itself from any small disturbance that unsettles it.

There you have it: safe, stable flight. The sort that you have come to expect as you settle back into your seat and sip that first drink of your holiday. But it would surprise you to know how long it took to achieve that and get it right in passenger aeroplanes. During one of British Airways' early route-proving flights to Bahrain with Concorde in 1976, while the aircraft was travelling at Mach 2 across the Mediterranean, a journalist turned to the late Sir George Edwards, the designer of the Vickers Viscount, Vanguard, VC-10 and the inspiration behind Concorde. The stranger said, between mouthfuls of caviar, "The amazing thing is, this all feels so normal."

"Yes." said Sir George, thoughtfully. "That was the difficult bit."

4

"You have control!"

Flying in a small dual-control light aircraft such as an Air Cadets Chipmunk in the 1960s enabled the aspiring young aviator to experience flying an aircraft for himself. The rear cockpit has all the controls and instruments of the front cockpit and they are inter-connected, so the young aviator is aware of levers and controls moving on their own, and in a way seemingly curiously unconnected with any instantaneous motion of the aircraft. After a few minutes climbing away from the airfield, a sudden and unexpected invitation comes through the headphones from the pilot in front.

"Would you like to fly the aeroplane?"

"Yes please, sir."

"Take hold of the control column with your right hand and follow me through - I'll show you how it works."

A small set of white knuckles in the rear cockpit, probably two sets if truth be told, grips the control column for dear life.

"If I pressure the column forward, the nose goes down, we descend and we speed up."

With hardly any movement from the control column at all, instead of pointing at the horizon, the aircraft dips down towards the green fields, the houses get bigger and the noise of the airflow outside increases. The cadet is also aware that the needles on at least a couple of instruments are moving where before they were stationary.

"If I pressure the control column backwards, the nose comes up, we climb and we slow down."

With a feeling of being pushed down into his seat, the young aviator sees the green of the fields ahead replaced by blue sky and things get quieter outside. The same couple of instruments reverse their previous excursions.

"OK now you try it on your own. You have control."

"I have control", says the cadet, remembering the echo of his briefing on the ground from a fatherly flight sergeant half an hour earlier. "If the captain says 'you have control' you must acknowledge it by saying 'I have control', and you must do the same when you hand control back. Why do we do that in the RAF? Because we lost lots of aeroplanes with both pilots thinking the other one was flying it, that's why, and Her Majesty, bless her, got a bit peeved after a while."

Two little sets of white knuckles clasp the control column even harder. A tentative little push, just a little push mind, sends the aircraft hurtling towards the ground. A pull in the opposite direction brings the nose above the horizon with a sickening lurch. The voice from the front: "Cor! My cheeks just landed in my lap. Where are yours, laddie? I have control for a minute."

"You have control, sir".

"The aeroplane doesn't need brute force. All that 'big men with hairy chests' stuff is just for the movies. It flies itself. You see we are back to straight and level now?"

"Yes, sir."

"Well, when it's trimmed straight and level it flies all by itself. Look!"

And a very surprised young cadet in the back sees two gloved hands waving above the pilot's head in the front cockpit. The aircraft flies on as before.

"So we need only the smallest force on the control column to make us do anything different from straight and level. Remember I said I was pressuring the controls, I said nothing about moving them. Hold the control column again, gently, just between the thumb and forefinger of your right hand this time. Tuck your other fingers out of the way. Got that? You have control."

"I have control, sir."

"Now, can you feel the rumble of the air over the control surfaces, in your thumb and fingertip?"

"Yes, sir!"

"That's coming into the control column through the cables that attach it to the control surfaces. Now you're really flying! Now, again, make sure just your thumb and forefinger are lightly grasping the column. With your forefinger, lightly pressure the control column backwards. Try not to move it, just put pressure on it and let the airflow do the work and look out to see what happens."

The Chipmunk's nose rises slowly above the horizon, and the rumbling in one young fingertip gets noticeably less as the speed reduces.

"Now pressure gently forward again with your thumb, and try to get the aircraft straight and level again, neither climbing or descending."

Not so easy. After five minutes of concentrated effort the nose is still either above or below the horizon, the Chipmunk gently porpoising across the countryside.

The voice from the front: "Not easy is it? But it comes with lots of practice. Remember you have to do that, as well as looking all around you to make sure you don't hit anything because that will ruin your whole afternoon and someone else's as well. Oh, and you have to know where you are, so you don't wander across London Heathrow in the rush hour. And you have to reply immediately to air traffic if they call you. Do you know where the airfield is?"

"No, sir."

"Fortunately I do, and I think we had better go back now. I have control."

"You have control, sir."

The Chipmunk rolls into a smart turn to starboard and turns through 160 degrees before rolling out on a heading into the setting sun. The cadet's headphones crackle with a different tone as the pilot presses the transmit button.

"Alpha 46 on recovery, ten miles to the north-east."

Immediately, the response. "Alpha 46, Runway 26 right hand, QFE 1007, three in the circuit." The controllers are always listening.

The voice from the front again: "Would you like to try a barrel roll on the way back?"

"What's that, sir?"

"I'll show you. It's a simple aerobatic manoeuvre, I'll talk you through it as I do it."

The cadet looks down for the waxed paper bag, thoughtfully provided by the man who fitted the parachutes, just as the Chipmunk does a steep turn to the left and another to the right.

"Before we can do aerobatics we need to do some checks - we call them the HASELL checks so we can remember them because the letters stand for each check. H is for height, which is 3,000 feet, OK for a barrel; A, airframe, the flaps are up, the wheelbrakes are off; Security, my straps are tight, are yours?"

"Yes, sir."

"You should say 'my straps are tight, sir' so that I know you have understood the question."

"Sorry, my straps are tight, sir!"

"Good, and the cockpit canopy is shut and locked." A white-gloved hand goes up to the yellow handle and gives it a push to be sure.

"Engine. Oil pressure is good, both magnetos are on, fuel we have plenty and its even tanks either side. Location is eight miles from base over open countryside and the last check is Lookout which I have been doing ever since I started those check turns and left you behind head down in the cockpit. Make you dizzy, did they?"

"A bit, sir."

"Always look out if you can. That's the checks complete. Here we go." The Chipmunk's nose dips below the horizon as the pilot opens the throttle and the engine roars to maximum.

"OK, a gentle dive and a bank to the left. Now I'm pulling up and rolling to the right so my wings are level as they pass through the horizon. Still pulling and rolling to the right as the nose comes way up above the horizon into the blue, feel that 'g'!"

The cadet cannot move; his body weighs two, nearly three times its normal weight as the aircraft pitches up and rolls to the right and the world goes ninety degrees, then a hundred and eighty degrees, topsy-turvy, green above, blue below.

"There we are, upside down! Still rolling to the right, but not pulling so hard now as the nose comes below the horizon, still rolling right and here comes the 'g' again as we go all the way round and.................there's right way up again! There, that's a barrel roll! Did you enjoy that?"

"Yes, sir. I think so." With a spinning head the cadet hears a chuckle from the front as the pilot throttles back and begins a steep descent towards the airfield. "I thought it was fantastic", says the cadet into his microphone. "My mum and my brother are never going to believe that."

From the 1960s to the present day, RAF Volunteer Reserve pilots have continued to give up their weekends to give cadets a taste of air experience, often a cadet's first flight ever. In the ten Air Experience Flights, as the organisations are called, up and down the country alongside the University Air Squadrons, nearly two hundred pilots fly cadets in the ninety-nine shared AEF/UAS aircraft. Cadet flying totals nearly 15,000 hours per year. The Chipmunk of the 1960s has been superseded, first by the Scottish Aviation Bulldog, and now by the Grob 115E Tutor, but the job today of the AEFs stays the same. It is to give 45,000 air-minded young men and women every year a taste of the sort of hands-on flying that some may never experience again during the rest of their lives. Equally important, the AEF operations make early and lasting impressions of safety, professionalism and discipline on all those youngsters who will choose subsequently to make aviation their life's work.

5

Solo but So High

Frequent flights gaining air experience in a Chipmunk helped the young aviator to build up a quick idea of how aeroplanes work and how they are operated. The next big leap forward was to learn to glide and to go solo. Gliding is serious flying, pure flying. It is serious and pure flying because gliders have no engine, and so the last option of the faint-hearted in a powered aeroplane (that of opening up the throttle and flying away from the ground if you get yourself into an uncomfortable situation) does not exist. Once they have been cast-off from their launching system, whatever form that may take, gliders come down. The skilful glider pilot can keep airborne longer than the unskilled one by making use of areas of lift in the air, but come down he or she will, eventually. Once committed to a landing, a glider pilot gets just one shot at it. That fact, above all others, makes gliding the ultimate serious aviation business.

It is perhaps surprising that at that time you could solo in a glider when you were sixteen years old, but not in a powered aircraft until you were seventeen. It was a great privilege in the early 1960s to be invited to go on a gliding course as a sixteen-year-old cadet and, after just four days and about twenty-five winch-launched three-minute flights in a two-seater glider, to fly solo and be airborne alone for the first time. That experience was one of life's forming moments because you, and you alone, were responsible for your continued existence. The alternative outcome was easily achievable, just by not doing what you had been told. On reflection many more people should go solo in a glider, especially those who have yet to discover both the value of listening carefully and of following instructions.

The gliders used by the Air Cadets in the 1960s were Kirby Cadet Mk3s, high wing, one seat behind the other, open-cockpit affairs that were stretched versions of a popular single seat design built before the Second World War. Aerodynamically they were not particularly efficient and came down rapidly after casting off from their launch, which meant that a lot of instructional points had to be packed into a very short space of time. For the cadet it felt a bit like drinking from a fire hose, while an unseen angry man behind yelled at you unreasonably all the way round the circuit about the huge quantities of water that you had missed. The Air Cadets' No. 1 Gliding Centre was at RAF Hawkinge, on the cliffs above Folkestone, Kent, where just twenty years earlier young men had fought the Battle of Britain in Hurricanes of No. 32 Squadron. Many of them had suffered much more than being yelled at, which rather put it all into perspective.

The initial familiarisation flight was quite terrifying. You were strapped into the front cockpit, little more than a seat with straps, thin plywood sides, an instrument panel and controls, and no canopy except for a small windshield ahead of you. Your only comfort was a mnemonic called 'CISTR', pronounced 'sister'. This stood for the vital checks:

Controls, Instruments, Spoilers, Trim and Release, all of which had to be checked without fail before committing to a launch. One cadet would hold the glider's wings level while the instructor asked for the winch cable to be attached, then for the slack in the cable to be taken up. Another cadet would wave an orange bat across his knees and the winch operator, half a mile away across the airfield, would slowly wind in the cable. As it tightened, the instructor would call "all-out" and the signalling cadet would start to wave the bat over his head. On seeing this signal the winch operator would open the throttle to wind in the cable, and the glider would leap forward and quickly into the air. Once airborne the glider adopted an attitude of about forty degrees nose up as it climbed through 200, 300, 400 feet. As it approached the point where it was getting overhead the winch it became progressively more difficult to keep the nose up, whereupon the pilot lowered the nose to slacken the cable slightly and then pulled the release toggle to jettison the cable. The cable was wound into the winch drum and then dragged back across the airfield by a four-ton truck to the launch point for the next glider. With a gentle breeze and a good winch operator (not too fast, not too slow), you would find yourself at 600 feet after launch, but descending relentlessly at about four or five feet per second. In the next couple of minutes you would turn left, away from the launch line (cross-wind), turn left again down-wind, all the while trying to understand what was being demonstrated and repeating it when shouted at to do so. Simultaneous with that, you had to adjust your path downwind (not too far away from the airfield, not too close either) so that, whatever areas of sink or lift you encountered downwind, you arrived abeam the launch point at 300 feet to turn left on to base leg. This allegedly positioned you nicely for a final turn into land at 150 feet, over the houses of RAF Hawkinge's long-suffering neighbours, to arrive back at the launch point.

Even flown by an instructor, it didn't look easy. The steep, hair-tearing climb during the launch was the first surprise and the speed with which things unfolded was the second. Each element was described by the instructor, but was finished long before his explanation. The cadet sat in the front, trying to understand what he was experiencing but which would not be explained to him until about five seconds later. The harder he concentrated, the more he seemed to miss other important things like how high the aircraft was, what lift or sink it was experiencing, and where it was in relation to the downwind target point in the sky that it had to reach if a safe landing was to be made. After a couple of flights, most cadets thought "I'll never be able to do this on my own in a year, let alone a week". The instructor's response to this reverie was to shout at you for having forgotten a vital action about which you had been "told time and time again, haven't you?" You had.

The first flying day's (Tuesday's) total was four launches and covered the effects of the controls. In a glider, because it travels slowly through the air, the effects of controls are more pronounced than on a powered aeroplane. The elevator, ailerons and rudder have, of course, their primary effects of controlling the glider's pitch (nose up and down), roll (one wing up, the other down) and yaw (left and right, side to side) just as on a Chipmunk, but they have secondary effects too that are not so apparent on powered aircraft. Take the rudder. A big bootful on a rudder pedal yaws the glider sideways, the nose swinging to the left or right. But a glider has a big wingspan and the wing that travels forwards during the yaw develops more lift because of its greater speed through the air. Similarly, the wing that goes backwards loses lift. The result is that the aircraft rolls as well as yaws, a right yaw gives a roll to the right and vice versa. If you want to see a pure yaw in a glider and nothing else, the rudder action has to be accompanied by just the right amount of opposite aileron.

And the ailerons that control roll have a similar secondary effect, but in the opposite sense. When you move the control column to the right to roll to the right, the right hand aileron goes up to reduce the effective curvature of that wing and lift is lost, causing that wing to go down. The left-hand aileron droops lower so the left wing develops more lift and that wing goes up. The primary effect of the aileron control is the roll that you would expect. But the secondary effect is that the up aileron also reduces the drag on the right hand wing and the drooped down aileron increases the drag on the left wing. As a result the aircraft yaws left, away from the roll. It is quite disconcerting to roll to the right and have the nose slice away to the left. You need a bootful of right rudder to counter that yaw and, once established in the turn with very little aileron, much less rudder. Thus all control movements are accompanied by small movements of other controls, which must be coordinated exactly for smooth flight. Get it wrong and not only will your flying look ragged but you'll also come down a lot faster because an unbalanced aeroplane has more drag.

All these novelties form the challenge that the young aviator faces as he or she attempts to learn to glide in a week. After that first flying day my logbook reveals that Wednesday was rained out, but Thursday packed in fifteen launches and covered almost the entire syllabus. Every flight covered one topic as well as practicing the launch, circuit planning and adjustment (done all the time, even during the topic demonstration) and of course the landing at the end. Three launches covered turns. Control column to the left. A yell from the back: "Too slow! And no rudder! Remember what you've been told!" Control column firmly to the left with enough left rudder to overcome the adverse yaw until a bank angle of thirty degrees, then hold off the bank and keep just a little rudder to go round. Then opposite aileron and rudder to straighten out of the turn. Quite good that! Then: "Laddie, if we keep on going this way, you may have your passport with you, but I don't, and I hate baguettes. The airfield is behind you and you are at four hundred feet heading for Boulogne! What are you going to do about it?"

Three more launches to practice stalls. An aircraft stalls when its forward speed is no longer sufficient to generate the lift it needs to overcome its weight and be able to fly straight and level. Aircraft stalls have absolutely nothing to do with engines. Ever! Despite what the media will say. Gliders can stall! As the aircraft flies slower and slower, the control column is held further and further back and the nose rises above the horizon as the pilot strives to maintain straight and level flight and the wing attempts to continue to develop enough lift to overcome the weight. Eventually, at some low speed, the flow over the top of the wing breaks down, the lift disappears and the aircraft stalls, pitching it nose down. Easing the control column forward unstalls the wing as the aircraft accelerates to normal flying speed and the houses below have become

*"... **you** may have your passport with you, but..."*

disconcertingly bigger as you regain level flight at normal speed; you can lose a lot of height in the recovery if you have been a bit slow off the mark. Altimeter needles stick, too, so temporary euphoria at an apparent moderate height loss after a stall can quickly turn into total despondency at the actual large height loss after you have remembered to tap the wooden instrument panel next to the altimeter. Forget to go for the wood and tap the altimeter itself and you get a knuckle full of glass, which can be fairly entertaining when added to all the other problems you are trying to sort out at the same time.

More launches, practicing stalls with one wing down. Keep the slip ball in the middle with the rudder because yaw is the father of the spin in a stalled aircraft. Spins are fun from 5,000 feet with a parachute, but their attraction palls at 500 feet with no time to use a parachute even if you had one, which you haven't. So unstall the wing, get flying speed, then pick up the wing.

And all the time, circuit planning, approach and landing. Downwind, past the takeoff point at 300 feet, keep the airfield within forty-five degrees down from the cockpit at all times. Don't know where forty-five degrees is? Dangle your arm out and look down it. Base leg turn, remember that rudder, finals turn at 150 feet, remember the rudder again, turn accurately so you don't lose too much height. Final approach at forty knots. Look for the stationary point ahead of you – that's where you are going to land, the airfield beyond the stationary point is moving up in the windscreen, the ground before it is moving down. And do remember to round out before landing. "Don't fly at the ground like that, laddie! The fact that you are going to die a split second before I do is of no comfort to me whatsoever. And if you break this nose skid I'll have you carving a new one from that tree over there!" The old airfield at RAF Hawkinge now has houses built on it, but is still recognisable. It has peculiarly treeless surroundings.

Launch emergencies. Practice cable breaks: "Don't forget to release the cable that's left attached to the aircraft. It's heavy and if you trail it over the neighbours they'll get the sulks and be round here, and I will personally introduce you to them!" Cable breaks at 500 feet (do a tight circuit). Cable breaks at 100 feet (land straight ahead). Cable breaks between 100 and 500 feet (lose height by doing S-shaped turns right and left and land straight ahead on the airfield. Try not to explore the hedge at the far end or, worse, land in the valley beyond.) "Someone did that last year. He's still down there, trying to take the glider to pieces and working out how to drag it back up the hill and he would love some company."

Circuits, circuits, relentless circuits. Right and left, some good, most bad and, most worrying of all, a total inability to tell what led to one being good and another bad. Horrendous landings. Rounding out a foot above the ground, but far too fast and ballooning up again to 100 feet far beyond the launch point, nose high and running out of speed, ideas, skill and luck simultaneously. On the next flight, arriving too slow over the hedge, keeping the nose up to stretch the glide in a desperate and futile attempt to reach the launch point and, as a result, stalling in from ten feet with a huge crunch. Invited to contemplate what will happen to self, should self be so unwise as to cause the skid to make a permanent impression on the bottom of one's instructor.

Friday, the last day. Most of your friends have gone solo, but you are back in the circuit with a new instructor who has clearly been briefed to confirm just how terrible you are. But wait, Mr Nasty has been replaced by Mr Nice. Four circuits, all quite good for a four-day veteran, certainly safe ones. There were three more to come, but they were to be different because Mr Nice is climbing out and is saying, mysteriously, "Stay there".

When it is clear that you are about to be sent off solo, the seriousness of your position suddenly dawns on you. Can you actually do this? What has caused this man, whose colleague has been yelling at you for the best part of a week for your incredible and, in his view, record-breaking lack of intelligence and ability, suddenly to assume that you are capable of taking a piece of Her Majesty's valuable property 600 feet over the heads of the good citizens of Folkestone for a few minutes without inflicting harm to yourself or to them? Has he taken leave of his senses? You decide not to argue.

Non-flying people often ask what a first solo in an aircraft is like. After many years of reflection, one has to conclude that it is very similar to a first sexual experience. You know it is going to happen sometime, the exact circumstances of it happening are invariably not quite as you had imagined they would be, and the whole thing is over so quickly that you are not sure of all the details, just that it went OK. It is also something that you must not do until you are absolutely ready for it. There is another parallel, too: three weeks later, when you have been repeating it constantly ever since that first time, you wonder what all the fuss was about. But there is, of course, one huge difference between the two: whereas a first sexual experience may be fuelled by alcohol, a first solo in an aircraft most certainly is not.

Sitting solo in the front cockpit of a tandem seat glider at the launch point feels just the same as sitting in it with the instructor behind you. The difference comes as you leap into the air on your own for the first time: it is quiet, uncannily quiet, in the back. And the aircraft goes up like a rocket and handles much more lightly without twelve stones of rampant criticism sitting in the rear seat. So your launch may give you another hundred feet of altitude or so, compared with what you achieved on every launch with Himself sitting in the back. Here all your circuit planning skills come to the fore, because there are no prizes for ending up over the landing point very fast and still at a couple of hundred feet, with the assembled ranks of instructors watching with curious detachment as you fly down the entire length of the airfield runway and disappear through the hedge at the far end. The alternative, just as easily attained, would be to misjudge it the other way, to undershoot on the approach and pass perilously close to the roofs of the houses bordering the airfield. One of these houses was a barber's shop. There is a picture somewhere of a Kirby Cadet glider perched on the roof of the barber's shop at Hawkinge with a chimney pot poking incongruously through the fabric of each wing.

Going solo has one startling revelation. In the RAF the captain of an aircraft is the boss, whatever his rank. While you can be told this and try to understand its implications, nothing can prepare you for the reality of what it means. Sitting in your cockpit, aged sixteen, awaiting a solo launch, you call for the winch cable to be attached to the nose of the glider: "Cable on, please!" The RAF air commodore who commands the UK cadet force, himself a distinguished fighter pilot, is visiting the gliding school for the day and happens to be within earshot. In his flying suit he runs over to pick up the cable, drags it across the grass to the glider and attaches it to the Ottfur release hook under the nose, giving it a tug to ensure it is attached. "Your cable is on, Sir!" he says to you. The air commodore calls you "Sir" because you are the captain of the aircraft. A working lifetime later, you wonder how much better large companies might perform if their culture was such that chief executives regarded the people at the sharp end of their organisations in the same way.

Forty years after the events above, Air Cadet gliding schools continue to flourish up and down the country. Twenty-seven schools (there would be more if the RAF could find more airfields to fly from) operate 160 gliders, most still winch-launched, but nearly half now the motorised self-launching type, the Vigilant. Between them, 700 volunteer instructors train 1,600 cadets on courses and send over 1,000 young men and women solo every year. Ask any airline pilot when he or she first went solo and they will often reply "when I was an Air Cadet, when I was 16". But they are only the tip of a very large iceberg. The important statistic is that, through the dedication of the instructors in the Air Cadet gliding schools over the years, tens of thousands of people in all walks of British life have had that unique experience of being up there, 'on your own'. Small wonder that air displays in the UK are the second most popular spectator event after football.

6

Across the World

For the really lucky air cadet in the 1960s the ultimate flying treat with the RAF was a trip across the world as supernumerary crew on an aircraft of Transport Command (as it then was) to and from one of its many worldwide destinations. In retrospect it was actually rather more than just a treat; it was nothing less than a very privileged look at a piece of aviation history, namely how long-range air transport operations were conducted before the development of all the equipment and facilities that we take for granted today. To an impressionable schoolboy the experience revealed the teamwork and personal qualities that a group of people needed if they were to take an aircraft full of passengers safely across the world.

At that time British armed forces were stationed all over the world with some of the largest numbers in the Middle and Far East. The people and equipment in these far-flung places needed constant support and re-supply, and the RAF had a large fleet of Comet (jet) and Britannia (turbo-prop) strategic transports to meet that need. It was good fortune indeed to be one of the few cadets who were selected each year to fly 'down the route' to RAF Changi in Singapore, a destination served three or more times a week from the UK. This was a unique opportunity because at that time the cost of travel to distant destinations was far beyond the means of ordinary people. A good working wage in 1962 was £20 per week or about £1,000 per year, and a return airline ticket to Singapore cost £400. There were no discounts and no bucket shops in those days. Cheap long-range air travel and student backpackers were definitely not yet invented.

First stop for the cadet was an afternoon visit to the RAF's Central Medical Establishment in London to be rendered immune to yellow fever, typhoid, tetanus and cholera, all at once. The experience usually also turned a cadet bright green on the train going home. Then, after a visit to RAF stores to get some tropical uniform that resembled sugar-sacks on a damp day, it was on to a train for the journey to Swindon for RAF Lyneham. In 1962 RAF Lyneham in Wiltshire was the home of the long-range transport force, No. 216 Squadron (Comets) and Nos. 99 and 511 Squadrons (Britannias). The Britannia operated a 'slip' system down the route to Changi, using crews from both squadrons. Cadets travelled on the same aircraft all the way to Singapore with one 'slip' crew after another, staying in Singapore with the second crew before returning with them as far as Aden and then continuing home with a third. It was the second crew that the cadet got to know best.

It was a very self-conscious cadet sergeant who presented himself at RAF Lyneham passenger terminal on a cold grey morning in July, resplendent in tropical uniform. Flight Lieutenant Gray's No. 99 Squadron crew quickly put me at ease because they too were in tropical uniform, although their suntans showed that they had used theirs before. They explained that I would not have much to do on their sectors because it was a VIP flight carrying the Air Officer Commanding-in-Chief Middle East and his wife back to Aden. As well as fifty passengers, Flight 6375 was fully loaded with freight for off-loading at the various destinations down the route. We took off at 1 p.m. into the grey murk and climbed to 21,000 feet over France for the five and a half hour first leg. The first surprise was how noisy the Britannia was. Four large turboprops make a great deal of noise and vibration, but this could be reduced a bit by the system (when it worked) that synchronised the propeller blades so that they all went round together. Even with that, one or two parts of the aircraft cabin had a 'node' of vibration and noise so that sitting at that spot for any time would give you a splitting headache. Britain to Singapore was about twenty-four hours flying, four 'legs' of six hours each with refuelling stops in between. For Service parents going on a posting with young children, it must have been something of an ordeal.

In those days the King of Libya was a good friend of Britain and the RAF had a staging post at El Adem in the Libyan desert about fourteen miles south of Tobruk. After glimpses through the cloud of southern France, then Italy and the Mediterranean in broad sunshine, El Adem was the first stop. It was a bleak place, just a tarmac runway and a few buildings in the middle of nowhere. We landed at dusk and it got dark during our two hour refuelling stop, with the desert stars an amazing sight right down to the horizon. The flight engineer supervised the refuelling to ensure that the right quantity of AVTUR was loaded into the correct tanks and he examined the engine oil levels for correctness and the airframe for signs of damage. The pilots and navigator went into Operations to study the weather before grabbing a quick meal. The air quartermasters supervised the off-loading of a small amount of freight, as likely as not spares to replace those that a previous Britannia had 'consumed' on a recent visit. In the aircrew cafeteria I had a short conversation with the chef. In less than half a minute he told me how much he was looking forward to going home and, without breaking eye contact, he killed two cockroaches. He then warned me that, when walking back to the aircraft, I should stay on the tarmac paths because the scorpions liked to sit on the sand at night. RAF people stationed at El Adem clearly went through some hardships for those stars.

By about half past nine local time in the desert night we were ready to go. Air Chief Marshal and Lady Elworthy returned to the aircraft in the station commander's car, the door was shut and the huge Proteus engines were started with the large blue electrical generator trolley for the long night flight over the desert to RAF Khormaksar in Aden.

While the Libyan government was a friend of Britain in 1962, the Egyptian government at that time (just six years after Suez) was not. RAF aircraft were not allowed to over-fly Egypt so the Britannia routed south, round the south-west corner of that country, before turning east towards the Red Sea. Navigation had to be spot on, and the navigator obtained regular position fixes from star positions that he first calculated approximately from a huge book of tables, then measured exactly with a sextant mounted in the flight deck roof. Three stars measured in two minutes gave him three position lines on the chart that hopefully crossed at one point - our position. If they didn't exactly cross, the three lines formed a 'cocked hat' shape, a small one if the navigator had a steady hand while 'shooting' the stars with the sextant, and your position was in the middle of the 'hat'. When the captain was absolutely satisfied that we were not about to cause an international incident by turning too soon, the aircraft turned to port across the Sudan, Eritrea and out into the Red Sea, then through the Straits of Bab el for a night landing at Khormaksar. We landed at nearly five in the morning local time, two o'clock Lyneham time and the crew had been on duty for nearly nineteen hours. Nowadays aircrews would never be routinely tasked with such a long duty time, but in those days it was accepted as normal - as these things always used to be until someone had an accident. Today's confidential human-factors reporting schemes for flight safety that can nip such unwise practices in the bud (see Chapter 17) were many years away. I said 'goodbye' and 'thank you' to a very tired crew.

Aden was searingly hot, even in the middle of the night. During refuelling the next crew arrived, Flight Lieutenant Don Salter's crew from No. 511 Squadron. With no VIPs on board things were a little more relaxed. The navigator gave me a headset and plugged me into the intercom, and from then I was invited on to the flight deck for all take-offs and landings, standing wedged behind the captain's seat. The Britannia was a complicated aircraft and its checklists were some of the longest in the business. The serviceability of one or two items like anti-icing was crucial to the safety and success of the flight, and high on the list for flying in the tropics was the special radar in the nose, the Cloud and Collision Warning Radar (CCWR), affectionately known as the 'cloud and clonk'. Whereas modern jets now cruise above the weather, the turboprop Britannia operated at 20,000 feet, right in the middle of it. In the tropics, cumulonimbus clouds ('bumblies') containing heavy turbulence and thunderstorms might go up to 40,000 feet. The CCWR was the aircraft's eye, spotting such weather up to sixty miles ahead and enabling the crew to route round the worst of it. But, true to Murphy's Law (see Chapter 8, "if something can go wrong, it will...") the CCWR failed soon after we had taken off as we were climbing out over the Arabian Sea. A quick conference ensued over the intercom, reviewing the weather forecast we had been given and some updates by radio that we had received since. The captain decided to continue into the clear early morning, the least risky time for thunderstorms, and we sent a Morse message to RAF Gan on the HF radio asking for a replacement radar set to be ready when we landed. The captain told me his decision would have been different on the next leg (Gan to Singapore) because of the certain risk of thunderstorms.

We headed south-east over the ocean towards the tiny island of Gan, six hours away at the southern tip of the 1,000-mile long Maldive islands chain. RAF Gan was sixty miles south of the equator, so as the aircraft crossed the equator the crew treated their young orange-squash-and-coffee-making colleague to a personal 'crossing the line' ceremony on the flight deck. This was carried out by the signaller, Master Signaller Bob Harvey, taking a break from tapping out position reports and de-coding weather reports as we flew along. The ceremony simply involved a small quantity of newly made orange squash finding its way down the back of a young cadet's neck. But it was the cue for a few minutes of unique flight deck humour, some of it now historic. Poking fun at the signaller's incessantly tapping Morse Code key, for example, there was much chuckling over the intercom when someone came up with: "She was only a signaller's daughter, but she Did It because her Dadda Did It".

Then, after five hours flying, navigated using a combination of Doppler-radar, dead-reckoning and astro sun and star-shots, RAF Gan replied to our calls on the VHF radio and used their direction finding equipment to give us a steer which was only two degrees different from the track we were flying. We flew a straight-in approach and landed at 2.45 p.m. local time. It was 9.45 a.m. back at Lyneham, the day after we had left; the young families and other passengers in the aircraft who were bound for Singapore had been travelling for nearly twenty-four hours.

Taxying in at Gan, I noticed a huddle of vehicles and tradesmen out to the left of the nose as the marshaller waved us in. With a smile, the air quartermaster (the aircrew category in 1962, now called air loadmaster), Sergeant (W) Sylvia Wapen, asked me if I would like to open the forward door of the aircraft. She knew I was in for a surprise because, as I did so, a figure shot by me carrying a black box, turned into the flight deck, pulled up a hatchway in the floor while the flight crew were still in their seats and disappeared into the equipment bay below. This was the replacement CCWR box that had to be fitted and tested satisfactorily before the refuelled aircraft could depart. There was a simple reason for the hurry. RAF Gan were so proud of their record that any section deemed to have delayed an aircraft on the route had to buy beer for the entire station in the messes that evening!

Gan looked like a paradise, at least to the visitor. Part of the Addu Atoll, it was a coral island surrounded by a green-blue sea and a reef. The island was inhabited only by RAF personnel, all of whom were on one-year unaccompanied postings. The local labour came to work from the neighbouring islands on boats, returning at dusk. The most popular activity on the station was scuba diving because the reef was host to thousands of species of brightly coloured tropical fish. Off the reef, a local man was employed to sit in a boat and watch for barracuda. On seeing barracuda he would ring a bell underwater to warn the divers who would get out of the water as quickly as possible. An RAF padre who served on Gan, the Reverend Gareth Jones, told me that from the shore the scuba divers appeared to pop up to the surface and walk across it to the nearest boat. When he had entered the Church, he said, he had never ever expected to see a man walking on water. The RAF Ministry had made his religious life complete, he reckoned, because he had seen men walking on the water lots of times at RAF Gan when the barracuda came in to feed.

Just two hours on the ground at Gan was followed by take-off for the dusk and night flight to Singapore. This time the repaired CCWR worked perfectly and came into good use as night fell and we dodged the huge thunderstorms over Sumatra. Tropical lightning all around you, above and below you at 20,000 feet, is quite a sight. I was kept busy serving soft drinks to the passengers, some of who were clearly unhappy in the very bumpy conditions. I felt quite useful explaining what I had just seen on the flight deck - the navigator, Flight Lieutenant Dick Thornborough, with his head buried in the rubber hood of the tiny CCWR screen saying to the captain "if you can come ten degrees to port now for thirty miles, captain, we can miss a big build-up ahead". And then the aircraft turning on to the new course after permission from the Sumatran air traffic controllers far below. With his protractor, rule and pencil exactly to hand in the darkness, the navigator quickly plotted the new course on the folded chart underneath all his scopes and instruments on the small, dimly-lit table. He was working very hard. There was no time for the gleeful banter he had enjoyed much earlier in the day over the Arabian Sea - all the maps thrown up in the air, with an "I don't know where we are and I don't CARE!" The lightning was always, reassuringly, kept in the distance.

The descent into Singapore was through thick cloud in the middle of the night. Only fleeting glimpses could be had of the city's lights as we flew round the instrument pattern before our final landing at RAF Changi and a warm welcome from the RAF air movements staff. RAF Changi was on the eastern tip of Singapore island and is now the site of Singapore's international airport, but in those days it was a very small airfield by comparison and with an RAF headquarters behind. It had one runway long enough for the Britannia, and that was crossed by a main road that was (hopefully) controlled by traffic lights. We landed there at ten to two in the morning local time, thirty hours after leaving Lyneham, and again Flight Lieutenant Salter's crew had been at work for nineteen hours since Aden. Nearly thirteen of them had been spent flying in challenging weather conditions with no navigational aids other than the sun and stars. We were all tired as we boarded the aircrew coach to the Air Transit Centre in Changi Creek. This was a beautiful place, a white painted tropical hotel on the banks of a creek surrounded by frangipani trees. It had been a Japanese officers' mess during the occupation of Singapore from 1941. Now it was host to RAF transit crews and passengers, the occasional lucky air cadet, dragonflies like small helicopters, amazing birds, flying insects the size of dinner plates, and the odd hornet. And chitchats: little lizards with suckers on their feet that ran up the walls and across the ceiling, hanging upside down over the slowly rotating ceiling fans... Mealtimes were anxious times, in case one fell. They often did, I was told with sometimes spectacular results, but they stayed glued to the ceiling for me, bless them.

The next two days exploring Singapore passed all too quickly for an occasional visitor like me, but it had clearly lost much of its attraction for those who had been there many times before. Meeting up with the crew at the appointed time revealed that the Britannia we were due to take back had had to return to Gan with, of course, an unserviceable CCWR. So we had an extra day in Singapore! We all made good use of it, but all too soon we were at breakfast in the hotel before leaving for the aircraft. The staff at the Air Transit Centre were wonderful and did their best to make our stay comfortable, but their grasp of English was not always perfect. Sylvia, the air quartermaster, ordered poached eggs on toast for breakfast and then, looking at her side toast and butter said, "And could I have some marmalade, please?" The captain had seen the blank look behind the waiter's eyes and said, "You are going to get marmalade on your poached egg!" "Oh no I'm not!" said Sergeant Wapen, and we all waited. When the poached egg arrived, guess what had been carefully spooned into its middle.

Back at the airfield the Britannia was serviceable and ready to go. XL635 "Bellatrix" looked good in the morning sun and I watched as the senior air quartermaster, Sergeant

Don Whitehead, calculated the load sheet for the flight. The length of runway available defined the safe take-off weight for the aircraft, and RAF Changi's runway was not long enough to permit a Britannia to be loaded to its maximum possible. The air quartermaster calculated the exact weight and centre of gravity position that resulted from the crew, passengers, freight and fuel we were carrying, and the co-pilot checked it. The weight, air temperature and runway length data were transferred to the aircraft's operating data charts to calculate the specific safety and decision speeds for the take-off. V_1 was the speed after which you were committed to complete the take-off because the runway wasn't long enough to stop after that. V_2 was the safe climb-out speed if an engine failed. In between was the speed at which the aircraft should be rotated, the nose-wheel lifted to take off, and the aircraft had to reach that speed comfortably before the end of Changi's runway. Water was injected into the turbines of the Proteus engines during take-off to cool them by a few degrees so that they could develop even more than their normally rated power without damage. The flight engineer, Master Engineer Pete Sinton, would ensure that water was flowing to all four engines and that all their revs, torques and temperatures were OK as the aircraft accelerated to V_1.

Checks complete, the aircraft taxied to the very end of Changi's runway. With clearance to take off from air traffic control, all four throttles were opened up to full power with maximum permitted numbers on the gauges. With water injection checked and double-checked for correct operation, and with the whole aircraft shaking with the engine power, the brakes came off. With the co-pilot Flight Lieutenant John Marshall flying the take-off, the heavy aircraft accelerated in the Singapore morning air and the end of the runway came ever closer. "Vee One!" called the captain and on we went. No choice now. One cadet, with just-taken 'A'-levels in pure and applied maths, peered over the captain's shoulder and wondered about all those calculations and all those lines on all those charts. "Rotate!" came the call as the target speed was reached and the Britannia flew - just as the numbers and piano-key runway bars disappeared under the nose. Everybody breathed again. "Coo, John!" said the navigator over the intercom to the co-pilot as the spinning nose-wheel thudded into its compartment and stopped below our feet. "Relying on the curvature of the earth, were you?"

And so the long journey home for the crew. Nineteen hours again for them between breakfast at Changi and collapsing exhausted at Aden. Thirteen of those hours dodging thunderstorms, coping with systems that went 'on the blink' (or went somewhere ruder if they were vital, like the Green Satin Doppler radar navigation system that measured, when it was working, the aircraft's ground speed and drift due to the high altitude wind). Thirteen hours, largely out of close radio contact with anybody, navigating by dead-reckoning using best-guess winds, the estimated positions then refined using astro fixes from the sun and stars. A standard of navigation so accurate that it was common to see, in mid-ocean, a few thousand feet above or below you, another RAF Britannia going the opposite way. That was a great treat because they were friends to talk to, in the middle of nowhere on clear VHF, and the two crews had vital information to exchange on weather and winds ahead of the other. At the end of nineteen hours, crashing out in the aircrew transit accommodation in Aden, recently sound-proofed and air-conditioned after a long battle with the Treasury ("Why do they need air-conditioning? Who do they think they are?"). And, after two days there, picking up another Britannia to fly home to Lyneham. Twelve days away from home (more if an aircraft had gone seriously unserviceable) to a welcome couple of days off, perhaps even coinciding with a weekend.

Then the crew would drift into the squadron to tackle the paperwork that had mounted up in their absence. And to see, in the Ops Room, the Perspex tasking board covered in Chinagraph pencil. The board told them that, because there was absolutely no other crew available, because of courses, postings and Royal Visit rehearsals, they were off down the route again to Changi the day after tomorrow...

On reflection, those routine global operations by the RAF and the airlines at that time, in piston and turboprop aircraft, were an astonishing achievement. Then only a few of the very newest transport aircraft were high-flying jets; the rest flew through the weather, not over it. There were no Global Positioning Systems (GPS) driven by satellites, or even long-range radio navigation aids. There were no inertial navigation systems and so no flight-management system that could be coupled with the autopilot to drive the aircraft along a pre-planned route. There was no Ground Proximity Warning System (GPWS) to warn a pilot of high ground as he approached to land in the dark or poor visibility, and most certainly no automatic landing system. A flight across the world then was something of a triumph, an intellectual triumph, by crews who pitted their wits and wisdom against the elements and whatever surprises and unreliability their 1950s technology had in store for them. As a team, they made it happen safely. The best crews, and I have tried to pay tribute to one here by recounting one journey in great detail, seemed close enough (on the ground, as well as in the air) to know what each of the others was thinking or wanting, without anybody ever having to ask.

7

GroundPounder

You could understand how any air cadet who enjoyed some of the experiences in the previous chapters might want to fly for a living, either in the Forces or with the airlines. For someone leaving school in the 1960s this might have been through RAF basic flying training on the Hunting Jet Provost, advanced flying training on the Folland Gnat, then weapons training on the Hawker Hunter followed by conversion on to some exciting operational type. Or, in civil aviation, training on Chipmunks and Piper Aztecs at the College of Air Training at Hamble, followed by conversion on to Vickers Vanguards of BEA or Boeing 707s of BOAC and a subsequent flying life centred around London Heathrow Airport. Not everyone, however, is lucky enough to be able to fly for a living. Even some of those who succeeded in being selected for training discovered that it was not for them when they got airsick, or when the knack of instrument flying eluded them for too long so that their sponsor's patience and budget ran out before they had time to develop the level of skill deemed necessary at that stage of their training. But the majority of hopefuls did not even get that far, because they failed during the selection process. Perhaps a vital O-level GCE eluded them, or they lost their temper with their team who were doing their best to cross a crocodile-infested river with two oil drums equipped for the task with only a piece of string, or they failed the medical. Top of the list of reasons for failing to make it into flying training was, however, a medical one. Eyes.

Casual observation of any group of professional pilots over the age of thirty reveals a large proportion wearing glasses. None of them, however, wore or needed glasses when they started flying training. A week after flying training started, it was OK. Lenses like Coke-bottle bottoms at the age of thirty-five, still OK. The RAF has even had a number of one-eyed pilots, one of the most recent resulting from a terrible accident with a shower tap in an aircrew transit block in Malta. But to be selected for sponsored flying training at the aircrew selection centres at Hornchurch or Biggin Hill, both eyes had to be good enough at the outset to enable the owner to fly without any optical correction. For many air-minded teenagers, keen to fly for a living and working hard on their homework in the evenings, the sudden descent into short-sightedness and NHS horn-rimmed glasses at school represented a huge disappointment. As did, in the 1960s, discovering that you were female. But life is full of such disappointments and it can be good to get some practice in early.

A great number of people then, previously having aspired to be a professional pilot, therefore have to settle for another type of career in aviation. Many are delighted to discover that a detached view of flying from elsewhere in the aviation profession does have some compensations. For example, rather than being limited like aircrew to the one strand of flying that had vacancies to match one's apparent abilities at the end of training (fighters, transports etc.), other careers can offer a wider ranging experience of different aircraft types and their operations. One option is aeronautical engineering, which offers a complete range of activities from the design and development of airframes, engines and avionics, to the improvement of safety during operations. Even as an engineer there can be many opportunities for some fascinating flying. More than one frustrated-pilot aeronautical engineer has found himself airborne in an early prototype, gazing at a set of gauge readings that show the drag to be ten percent greater than calculations predicted. Or strapped into an ejection seat in an operational type, trussed in a g-suit, bone-dome and oxygen mask, trying to investigate a fault that cannot be reproduced on the ground and which seems only to occur at 300 knots and in a tight turn at 3g or more. One young female engineer found herself in just such a situation one afternoon. Given her previous lack of success at being selected for aircrew, she thought somewhat justifiably to herself: "How on earth did I get here?"

The answer, of course, is: 'You got here because many people just like you made it possible. As you, in turn, are making it possible for many more like you to follow in your footsteps; faster, higher, more efficiently or more safely.' As we have seen, it has been the quests for more efficiency and safety that have been the driving forces of aeronautical effort over the past fifty years. That all sounds rather grand, but the reality is that people have learned the hard way and have simply used their wit and wisdom to try to prevent others learning the same thing in the same way. Wit and wisdom are qualities to be found throughout the aviation profession; the issues are so serious that a dry cynicism, and an irreverent disregard for anything and anybody that seems to stand in the way of progress, seem to be the rule.

Top of the aviators' 'to-be-disregarded' list are people who do not fly. The general term for them is 'blunties', as in 'those at the blunt end'. But pilots on one RAF fighter squadron had a particularly apt description of the genre: they called them GroundPounders. Anyone who worked in station headquarters was definitely a GroundPounder. Whether the pilots imagined this ground pounding was with actual fists, or simply with feet, was not clear. One month the squadron had been hosting rather too many visits from the local ladies knitting circles and the like, something they enjoyed doing, but too much of it had caused the squadron to get behind on its training programme. The Boss had very wisely said "no more" for a bit, but the following week the squadron engineering officer received a request from a civil servant in Yorkshire, one of the silent many who manage the buying of all the spares and ground equipment for the RAF and who get value for money for the Treasury. Could he please visit the squadron? The Boss said "No". The engineering officer protested: "But just this one, Boss, he does a lot for us". The Boss still said no. "But Boss, you've *got* to allow just this one, look at his name". His name was Mr G. Pounder.

In due course Mr Pounder arrived, a delightful man, and the squadron put on the works for their guest. The pilots made a huge fuss of him, sat him in a cockpit, showed him all the kit. To this day he will never have known the reason was his name. For them he was GroundPounder personified and, if he reads this, I hope he doesn't mind.

Mr Pounder's visit, however, paid some significant dividends in defence expenditure.

46

He was appalled at the casual way some of the simpler ground equipment was treated by the squadron's groundcrew – ladders dropped, rather than placed on the ground, etc. He asked if anyone knew how much various items cost the defence budget and of course nobody did. But he knew to the nearest penny and his information shocked the equipment's users. Over coffee it was decided that, where possible, new equipment would bear a label showing what it cost. The new labels had a sobering effect on the equipment's users. "A thousand pounds for *that*?" A few months later there was a marked difference in the way equipment was treated and the squadron's consumption rate of aircraft ladders and other items had reduced dramatically.

Sometimes, however hard the GroundPounders work to support the flying, all their efforts are in vain. In the RAF Far East Air Force in the late 1960s, a squadron of Whirlwind helicopters was having a difficult time with spares. Big spares were all right: demand a gearbox or a replacement engine and one would appear by way of an Air Support Command Britannia within a week or ten days. But little things just seemed not to appear. The little fasteners that held the flexible lining to the helicopter's cabin wall used to break and replacements came in little boxes of twenty. One squadron had these fasteners on order for weeks and, pending their arrival, aircraft linings had to be attached to the cabins with bits of string where the fastener had broken. This was perfectly safe, but it was unsightly, unprofessional, and un-nerving too for any passengers flying with the squadron for the first time. The suppliers knew about the urgency of the need because the squadron's engineers reminded them daily, but lack of spares was not grounding an aircraft and only that seemed to attract interest at high level back in the UK. Eventually the supply staff received a message about the requested spares from the UK: there was no stock, and new ones were going to have to be manufactured. The estimate was six months!

The squadron flew on, with even more bits of string, for six months. The engineers still gave the supply staff their daily reminder, but their heart was no longer in it after a while. Eventually the engineering officer received a phone call, curiously down beat, from the chief supplier. "We have got your 26DK/etc. etc." (items were always referred to by their stores reference number). "You had better come over to the Supply Squadron." "No need for that," said the engineer, "just put it on the afternoon wagon and send it over." "No," said the supplier, "there's a problem. I think you had better come over here and have a look."

The engineer got into the squadron Mini and drove round the airfield until he came to the Supply Squadron building. On the step to meet him, wearing hangdog expressions, were all the suppliers he knew. "Come and see this," they said and led him into the yard. In the yard, newly delivered by ship from the UK, was a huge box about eighty feet long, containing a complete wing for a four-engined Shackleton maritime reconnaissance aircraft. Not a fastener for a Whirlwind helicopter in sight. What had happened was that, somehow, the stores section/reference number for the fasteners had been written down or copied wrongly somewhere along the supply chain. As a result, Messrs Avro Aircraft Ltd had built, to special MoD order and at huge expense, a complete new wing for an entirely different aircraft, all because one letter or number was wrong! Ordered again, properly, that very afternoon, the required fasteners were on a Britannia and with the Whirlwind squadron the following week. Supply Squadron bought beer in the messes for weeks and weeks on the strength of that one. History does not record if the new Shackleton wing was ever used before the aircraft type was retired from service, but the Law examined in the next chapter would predict not. Later that year the RAF Supply staffs fired up their first computer and after that they never looked back. With the computer, the section/reference numbers had self-checking digits and an incorrect entry would be immediately spotted and rejected. Never mind speed, efficiency, stock-level modelling and all the usual arguments in a cost-benefit case for computers - eliminating mistakes like that Shackleton wing must have saved the country millions.

If the computers could be persuaded to avoid mistakes, however, humans carried on as before. In the early 1970s, NATO adopted a policy of dispersing its aircraft around their bases during alerts to avoid the risk of their being picked off by surprise strafing raids while parked in straight lines, as had happened during the 1973 Yom Kippur War. One RAF fighter squadron had great difficulty complying with this order because the dispersals on its airfield were asphalt. This surface was fine for the Canberras that had once dispersed there, but asphalt was too soft for the heavy Lightning with its narrow high-pressure tyres. Taxying across it was OK, but parking on it was not because the aircraft sank quickly up to its axles. The solution was large mild steel plates, three for each dispersal, placed where the nosewheel and mainwheels were supposed to be when the aircraft was parked on a safe heading (i.e. with its weapons pointing at something arable rather than residential). Each plate spread the load of the wheel. So the squadron requested enough steel plates to equip all its dispersals, only to have the demand refused point blank by Headquarters Strike Command. Because it was too expensive. After a lot of argument, during which the comparative costs of a few mild steel plates and the effectiveness of one fifth of the nation's air defences were enthusiastically discussed, the answer was still 'No'. With the squadron unable to fulfil its NATO requirement to disperse and RAF Strike Command unwilling to supply the means, the squadron's pilots and engineers contemplated doing what Service people usually do: having a whip-round to buy the plates themselves. But in their final letter Command HQ softened slightly and said that they could only provide the steel if "a specific operational exercise was cited". Ever equal to a challenge, Flying Officer Greg Harker, the squadron junior engineering officer, concocted a letter around a mythical project called the 'Special Operational Dispersal Of Friendly Fighters' and this was duly sent off. Lo and behold, the following week the squadron received all the steel plate it needed for its dispersals. To this day nobody knows if HQ RAF Strike Command ever realised that the bogus special project, cited so carefully by the squadron's engineers, contained a distinctly coded message in its title.

For the most part, however, support for RAF flying operations worked really well by the 1970s. In one engineer's view, the effectiveness of the RAF Lightning force depended greatly on the initiative and flexibility of the Supply Branch. A good example of this was provided one bitterly cold Friday afternoon one January when a squadron

"... heavy things on asphalt need steel plates..."

suddenly needed an Air Turbine Gear Box (ATGB) to replace a new one that had failed while being test run on an aircraft being prepared for an operational deployment to Cyprus the following Monday. By 2.30 pm the base was in a blizzard and the only Lightning ATGB in Britain, which weighed over 300 lb in its box, was in a warehouse at RAF Stafford, a hundred miles away across the Pennines. But that replacement ATGB appeared in the hangar beside the stricken aircraft at 4 pm that afternoon. It arrived through the blizzard in a No. 33 Squadron Puma helicopter, the last RAF aircraft movement in the UK that day. The RAF Supply organisation had understood the operational need and had responded accordingly. Then came the engineers' turn. Removing the No.2 engine, removing and re-fitting an ATGB, refitting the engine, test running it, flight-testing the aircraft etc. could typically take a squadron up to four days. The job was done in two, and the Lightning left for Cyprus, in another blizzard, on time on the following Monday morning and rendezvoused with its tanker over the Channel. The RAF support team really worked that weekend and from all accounts it hasn't stopped since

Even GroundPounders can make a difference. Everybody connected with aviation, however remotely, has a role to play in making it happen, in improving its safety and reducing its cost. That is why it is possible now to fly with a profitable airline from London to Glasgow for less than a subsidised train fare and in a fraction of the time. That is a substantial technical and economic achievement, but it is also an amazing achievement in human terms. Which is why this book celebrates the wisdom and spirit of some of the people who have made that possible over the past fifty years.

8

Murphy's Law states...

Have you ever driven round the M25 motorway west of London on a foggy weekday December morning at about 8 a.m.? 'Driven' might be putting it a bit strongly, because for the most part on such a day the traffic on that stretch is either stationary for long periods of time or travelling at a crawl. On the traffic news broadcasts, BBC Radio is telling not only of the jam that you are sitting in but of countless others. The railways are not working that morning either because the lines are slippery or the signals have failed, and the London termini are in chaos. As you sit in your car, pondering this mayhem and with little to smile about except the wild imagination of one of Terry Wogan's slightly demented listeners on Radio 2, one revelation suddenly strikes you as you see lights through the murk. Heathrow is operating normally. A constant stream of airliners of all sizes, from a KLM twin-prop commuter airliner from Rotterdam to a British Airways Boeing 747-400 from Brisbane (last stop Singapore, thirteen hours ago), whistle overhead and descend about three minutes apart down the glide-slope of Runway 9L for a safe touchdown in London. Landing in freezing fog? No problem. So while 'London to Glasgow for less than a subsidised train fare and in a fraction of the time' is a great technical and human achievement, there is another factor that really underlines the triumph of technology over nature that is air travel. All this you can do in safety, even in the freezing fog. Not in perfect safety, because there is no such thing, but at the socially acceptable level of safety that we enjoy in commercial air transport. It is a level of safety that has been achieved in spite of a well-known natural law that goes along the lines: 'if something *can* go wrong it *will* go wrong, some time'.

'Newton's Law of Cussedness' it used to be called by the engineering fraternity, but in more recent times the principle of 'if something can go wrong, it will' has been widely recognised and is known by the much more succinct title of 'Murphy's Law'. Well established in aviation, there are even corollaries to it such as Sod's Corollary to Murphy's Law - 'when that something *does* go wrong, it does so at the worst possible moment'. But 'Murphy's Law' is not named, as some suppose, because some wag decided to have a tilt at Irish logic. Its origins are firmly in aviation because it is named after Captain Edward A. Murphy, USAF, an engineer at Edwards Air Force Base California in 1949, and his story is recounted in a comprehensive internet website, 'www.murphys-laws.com'. Captain Murphy was working on US Air Force project MX981, which was designed to investigate how much deceleration a human being can withstand in a crash by firing him in a rocket-powered sled along the ground and braking it in an instant. One day, finding a component wired wrongly, he cursed the individual responsible and said: "If there's any way to do it wrong, he'll find it". The contract manager kept a list of 'laws' and added this one, which he called 'Murphy's Law'. At a press conference soon afterwards, Dr J. P. Stapp, the Air Force doctor who rode the rocket sled through its eye-popping 40g deceleration, paid tribute to the safety record achieved during the project and put it down to a "firm belief in the principles of Murphy's Law and the need to try to overcome them". From then on the Law was never called anything else and in the aviation world it has focused the minds of all designers, engineers, pilots and other aircrew ever since. It also enjoys popular usage because, with its corollary, it explains exactly why toast not only can be dropped, but also why it invariably lands butter-side-down.

On occasion, Murphy asserting his Law has been particularly painful. In March 1957 a Blackburn Beverley freighter on a flight from its home airfield at RAF Abingdon to Malta experienced engine problems soon after take-off and tried to return to Abingdon. It did not make it - the aircraft crashed on to the nearby village of Drayton and killed fifteen of the seventeen in the aircraft and two people on the ground. Two of the aircraft's engines had been starved of fuel because a non-return valve in the fuel system, a valve that can only pass fuel in one direction, had been fitted back-to-front. Nowadays, doubtless, the poor soul who fitted the valve would be prosecuted to within an inch of his life and, having done that and noted the appropriate sources for compensation, the world would be very tempted to carry on smugly. In those days, too, the tradesman and his supervisor were court-martialled, but they were subsequently found 'not guilty' of the main charge. A far more important action that resulted was that airworthiness design standards were changed so that the threads at either end of all such valves manufactured since are now made totally different from each other. Items like a non-return valve simply cannot now be assembled in the wrong sense. Nevertheless you would be amazed how many people have still tried to do so in the forty-seven years since, most realising their mistake after looking at the manual and quietly and ruefully thanking those who had gone before them and made it impossible. Yet some have actually *complained* about not being able to fit such valves the wrong way round, before having life's (and death's) realities pointed out to them. In aviation there is a saying that there are two types of people, 'those who have, and those who will'. The objective when designing aircraft or the rules for operating them is to make the unwise or dangerous action impossible or at least crushingly difficult for those who even try. But even then, against all the odds, some will succeed. A new piece of equipment has to pass the critical test: 'Is it Murphy-proof?' and much of the designer's intellect is directed towards ensuring that it is just that.

Sometimes Murphy acts to amuse, even to tease. Engines, for example, *can* go wrong so they *will*. Lord Hives, chairman of Rolls-Royce the aero-engine manufacturer, was once asked why he always flew in four-engined aeroplanes. He famously replied that it was because there were no five-engined aeroplanes. Today, engine reliability is such that aircraft can fly safely for long distances on just two engines, but in the days of piston engines Lord Hives had a point. Engine shut-downs used to be commonplace. Moreover, when a piston engine was shut down and the propeller was 'feathered' (blades turned end-on to the airflow) and stationary, everybody could see out of the windows that it had stopped working! Another RAF Beverley was involved in an incident one day when it lost an engine en route from Singapore to Manila in the Philippines, bound eventually for Hong Kong. One of the passengers seated in the tail boom was the RAF station's Roman Catholic padre, who loved flying and got airborne at every opportunity. Unfortunately, some twenty minutes after the engine was shut down, another started to overheat and the air engineer advised the captain that, if its temperature continued to rise, it too would have to be shut down. The Beverley could not maintain height on two engines out of four, so the captain ordered that all the passengers and supernumerary crew in the tail boom should move forward on to the flight deck. If they had to ditch, that was the safest place for everyone to be. When the passengers arrived, having climbed down into the hold from the tail boom and then up the steps to the flight deck, the captain briefed them on their situation. Spotting the padre, the captain said that he was very pleased to see him and that "Father, this is probably an appropriate time for you to do something religious". The padre did not hesitate for a second; he knew what to do. He removed his hat and took a silver collection from all the petrified souls gathered around him on the flight deck. It must have worked because the aircraft went on to land safely in Manila where repairs to the engines were carried out before the aircraft flew on to Hong Kong. Flushed with his success as a force to be reckoned with for flight safety, the padre acquired a flying suit in Hong Kong and wore it proudly for the journey back to Singapore, complete with his dog collar. The armed US Air Force personnel who guarded the aircraft as it staged back through Saigon were at a loss to understand what this apparent aircrew clergyman was doing near an aircraft, let alone in a flying suit, and challenged him as he approached the aircraft. "Just what is your role, Sir, in the crew of this airplane?" they demanded. The padre had no hesitation again and looked them straight in the eye. "I am the Maker's Representative", he said.

When a single-engined aircraft such as a fighter or a trainer suffers an engine problem, the result can often be the loss of the aircraft. And Sod's Corollary to Murphy's Law usually means that such problems occur at awkward moments where a forced landing is impossible – at low level, or at 3,000 feet above a nice long runway. "Hang on," you might think, "a decent height above a long runway, surely that's ideal?" The trouble is that, at that precise moment, Sod's Corollary has just come into play: that nice long runway, far below you, will have just been blocked by an aircraft with a burst tyre.

Murphy's Law, 'if something can go wrong, it will', has brought about its own form of defensive behaviour that becomes second nature when operating aircraft, a behaviour best summed up by another flight safety slogan: 'Don't Assume – CHECK!' Nothing can be taken for granted, ever, and being aware of that has saved many a life. Years ago a British Airways Trident airliner had an engine failure as it landed at a regional airport in Ireland. The damage was extensive and it was decided that, if possible, the aircraft would be flown back to London empty on the two good engines instead of the usual three, by a special crew. The two-engine ferry on a Trident was a special operation needing great care and British Airways' performance engineers soon arrived on the next Trident from London to assess the situation, de-mobilise the failed engine and do the sums. Their calculations showed that the airport's runway was so short that, taking off on two engines, the Trident's all-up-weight would have to be limited to much less than its normal operating value. This meant that, as the aircraft stood, it could only carry just enough fuel to reach Heathrow, but not to go-around and divert if Heathrow became unavailable for any reason. This was clearly unacceptable, so the performance engineers looked around for weight that could be removed in order that the aircraft could take the extra 2,000 pounds of fuel it would need to give it diversion capability from Heathrow. They decided that the galley and all its equipment would suffice as it weighed slightly more than 2,000 pounds. They left instructions for the local maintenance company to remove the galley and equipment and for the extra 2,000 pounds of fuel to be loaded. They then departed to the hotel for an early start in the cool morning air the next day.

The next morning the flight test crew and the engineers arrived at the empty aircraft to find the galley and equipment duly stripped out, as per instructions, and the fuel gauges reflecting the extra tonne that had been put in. The local base engineering support had worked hard overnight, but there wasn't going to be any in-flight coffee on the way to London. All was ready for the flight, the temperature was nice and low for the marginal take-off on the short runway (jet engines produce more thrust in low air temperatures) and everybody was strapped in. But before the two serviceable engines were started, however, one of the BA engineers had an uneasy feeling. Where *was* the galley and equipment? He hadn't seen them on his way to the aircraft. There wasn't a pile of boxes under a tarpaulin anywhere nearby and he hadn't seen anything in the small British Airways equipment area either. Rather than assume, he decided to check so he asked the captain to hold the engine start for a couple of minutes and for the steps to be rolled back into place. On the ground, the starter crew were new on to the morning shift and had no idea where the stuff had gone. Standing on the tarmac, with the aircrew at the top of the steps impatient to start but with a huge 'Don't assume, CHECK!' lit up in his head, the BA engineer followed his instinct. He opened the hatch to the Trident's baggage and cargo hold to look inside. There, neatly stowed with regulation lashing tape, were all the galley units and equipment from the cabin upstairs, all 2,000 pounds weight of them.

Back in the 1940s and 1950s the RAF had many more aircraft and pilots than it does now, and sometimes they were put to more social than military use in ways that nowadays would be most unacceptable. On one such occasion, a parade was to be held at RAF Duxford to say farewell to a departing senior officer from No 11 Group of Fighter Command, Air Vice-Marshal Victor Bowling. The station organised a formation flypast of Vampire fighters to roar over the saluting base as he took the salute, and of course the formation had to be in the grand man's initials. The squadrons practiced for weeks with two formations, one for each letter, and gradually, with 'whipper-in' aircraft flying above and below the formations, got them into reasonable individual shape and alongside each other for the day of the parade itself. On the great day, with the parade at 'present arms', the band playing and the grand old man saluting, the giant formation of seventeen aircraft approached the saluting base from the right direction and on cue (itself an achievement) just as one of the pilots got a fuel pressure warning and an engine wind-down causing him to drop smartly out of the formation. Yes, Sod's Corollary had asserted itself and the middle aircraft of the 'B' formation had failed at the worst possible moment. History tells that the old man was not at all pleased at the giant 'VD' that roared overhead. Whether or not the Air Vice-Marshal understood the intricacies of Murphy's Law, he must surely have smiled at the memory a few years later when Mr Duncan Sandys, the Defence Minister, observed ruefully: "It's only when you're spouting that you get harpooned".

Ceremonial parades and flight safety 'Murphys' seem to have such an irresistible attraction for one another that it is surprising that officialdom hasn't spotted the link and banned the two together. An RAF base in Singapore in the 1960s was the scene of yet another embarrassment. The commander-in-chief was visiting a new support helicopter force that had been assembled at RAF Seletar to deploy to assist the Sultan of Brunei who was facing a rebellion. All personnel, with the exception of those involved in training flying which took priority, were ordered to parade for the occasion. As it happened, the parade was drawn up right in front of the helicopter dispersal at the same time that a training sortie was scheduled for XG475, one of the Belvedere helicopters in the special force.

As the parade had formed up and was standing easy, the helicopter crew sauntered out of the squadron crew-room and towards the aircraft, grinning happily at the sea of less

"For Heaven's sake don't clap..."

fortunate faces in their smart tropical uniforms. The Belvedere was the first of the RAF's twin rotor helicopters and was a sort of anorexic Chinook. Like the Chinook it had a wheel at each corner, but unlike that aircraft it did not sit parallel with the ground – the nose was proud in the air and the pilot needed an eight-foot ladder to climb up into the cockpit. As well as for access, the ladder was an essential item of safety equipment because the Belvedere had a problem. The aircraft was started by means of an innocuously sounding (but far from harmless) substance called AVPIN. AVPIN is the RAF name for iso-propyl nitrate, a liquid monopropellant. Sprayed into the combustion chamber of a starter motor and ignited, this liquid combined its explosive (the propyl) and its oxidant (the oxygen in the nitrate): its spray would burn continuously into a high pressure gas that discharged through a turbine, so spinning up the main gas turbine engine of the helicopter and enabling it to start. The problem with the Belvedere was that, occasionally, the exhaust holes in the starter's combustion chamber would become blocked and then, instead of producing a hot gas stream, the starter motor would explode as the accumulated pool of AVPIN liquid detonated. So for a while, before the problem was solved, the pilot's ladder became an essential piece of safety equipment for Belvedere operations. It was essential because it would remain against the cockpit door as an escape route while the pilot would do all his cockpit checks and start the engines. If, when the pilot pressed the start buttons, the starters and engines went 'whoosh' as advertised, the ladder would be taken away. If either starter went 'BANG', however, the pilot would descend the ladder as quickly as he could and, in the finest traditions of the Service, run away bravely while people who were better equipped than he would deal with the consequences of the explosion.

In front of this large parade at RAF Seletar the ladder was solemnly placed up to the cockpit and the pilot went about his checks as the crewman settled himself in the rear door at the back. With the cockpit checks complete the first engine started properly at the rear of the aircraft and the rotors began to turn. But the second start, of the forward engine, produced quite the largest bang that anybody had ever heard from a Belvedere. The whole parade cheered as the pilot shot down the ladder with his arms and legs going like a rotating swastika until he hit the ground and the swastika became the motion of choice for running away. To the distaste of the parade commander, who was facing the wrong way in a forlorn attempt to get the parade under control, they cheered all the harder as a tongue of flame licked around the foot of the front engine, behind the cockpit. The ground crewman did his best to tackle the fire with a small trolley extinguisher, but he was relieved to be joined by the fire engine positioned nearby whose crew quickly made foam. However, the turning rotors prevented the fire tender getting close enough and the foam fell short of its target. The fire crew shut down the foam and the helicopter crewman succeeded in reaching into the burning helicopter and shutting off the fuel to the rear engine so that the rotors would stop. Once they had stopped, the fire tender was able to back in much closer and out went the order "make foam" again. Unfortunately, this time the foam simply bellowed out of the back of the fire tender and enveloped it in a huge beige puff-ball, to the delight of the parade which by this time was out of control with Keystone Cops syndrome. One of the parade's more responsible members had broken ranks to run to a phone to raise the alarm. He reported a fire on the helicopter dispersal, but the local civilian operator said in a bored tone, "Yes, I know, the C-in-C's here and he always pulls a false fire alarm when he's around" and hung up! The air traffic controller in the tower did, however, hit the fire alarm and the rest of RAF Seletar's fire engines responded and raced up to the aircraft to more cheers. With hoses out and water and foam at last beginning to flow on the furiously burning Belvedere, the fire commander angrily turned his attention to the original foam tender hiding in its foam puffball and ordered its crew to "get it out of here". They duly drove off - but straight over the hoses of the newly arrived fire engines. The hoses burst and all the water went everywhere except where it was needed. The parade was ecstatic and began to break up in disarray. It was not so much a case of going 'absent without leave' as it was of people sidling quietly off the parade to fetch their cameras, and then sidling back on to it again as quickly as possible to record the spectacle! They did not have long to wait for the next debacle. The station Tannoy system had ordered that all personnel should place every available fire extinguisher in a police Land-Rover outside station headquarters and this was quickly done. The Land-Rover sped to the scene and screeched to a halt. As it did so, all the fire extinguishers inside fell over and went off, and a second vehicle at RAF Seletar that afternoon became enveloped in its own personal foam puff-ball. The parade loved it and produced a final wave of that uniquely British indication of loyalty and support that can be so misunderstood - by one's headmaster when one is young, and by other nations when one is older - ironic cheers. The cheers were by this time mixed with a melodious and particularly well sung musical round from across the ranks, to the tune of 'London's Burning':

"Seven-five's burning,
Seven-five's burning,
Call the engines!
Call the engines!
Fire, fire!
Fire, fire!
Sack Wingco XX! (the name of the hapless parade commander)
Sack Wingco XX!
Seven-five's burning,
Seven-five's burning…"

Eventually the burned-out nose of the aircraft fell off and the front of the Belvedere was smoking ash, but at least the fire was out. Only the back end of the aircraft was left, its rotors drooping sadly towards the ground. And with every fire appliance on the station now discharged, the airfield had no fire cover and so the visiting C-in-C's aircraft was grounded and couldn't leave. The C-in-C had to return to HQ Far East Air Force at Changi in a staff car after what must have been a most memorable visit. Years later, many of those on parade that day declared it to be the defining moment of their Service career. The day Sod's Corollary to Murphy's Law struck - with an audience to appreciate it.

9

Firing Up

The story of the Bristol Belvedere and its AVPIN explosions illustrates one of the biggest problems in aviation: starting the engines. One RAF pilot, having given control to a passenger sitting in the co-pilot's seat and feeling a bit miffed at how this complete novice (a female novice at that) was doing rather well, observed that "any fool can fly - it's just that hardly anybody can land". If only it was that simple. Many experienced pilots, quite able to fly and land their aeroplane, find it a great challenge to start the thing. As we will see in Chapter 11, some face an even bigger struggle when stopping it.

In the earliest days, piston engines on the first aircraft were hand-cranked to start, rather in the manner of the starting handle that used to be a feature of motor cars, until a Mr Issigonis decided to turn the engine sideways in the Mini so that a starting handle wouldn't fit. Then 'propeller-swinging' came along, whereby, once the pilot had activated the ignition system ("Contact!"), some brave soul would step up to a live and fully primed engine and swing the propeller through a compression of a cylinder in the firm hope that it would fire in the right sense (i.e. when the piston was over top-dead-centre) and the engine would start to run forwards, not backwards. This technique is widely referred to as the 'Armstrong' method, and generations of young pilots of light aircraft have revered the inventiveness of the supposed 'Mr Armstrong' until they have twigged from their aches and pains after a day's helping at the flying club that a person actually needs a very strong arm to do it and the penny has dropped. In fact, you need more than a strong arm. You also need the wit to realise that the job is best done by *stroking* the propeller through its motion, rather than pulling it through the swing by wrapping your fingers round the blade. This is because, if the cylinder fires prematurely and back-fires, having your fingers curled around the blade will result in, at best, broken fingers and at worst, no fingers at all. Last, the swinging action itself has to be almost a poetic ballet movement that involves the swinger leaving the area of the propeller immediately. If the engine does start, being next to a rotating propeller is not a good thing.

All this sounds jolly easy. In fact, getting exactly the right mixture of fuel and air primed into the engine is no mean feat. If the mixture is right, but the engine doesn't start because the spark from a cylinder is poor, or the propeller swing is poor, further swings will enrich the mixture with fuel and the engine will then firmly refuse to start because it is flooded. Switching off the magneto ignition and flicking the propeller backwards may, if you are lucky, purge the engine of its temporary richness and enable you to start all over again, but from a point where you are considerably more tired than you were when you first tried. And so it goes on. Millions of people go to air shows every year, ostensibly to see old aircraft flying. But when you have spent twenty minutes in front of a crowd trying to get your old aeroplane started so that it can meet its take-off display slot time, without success, the gleeful smiles from the crowd sometimes convince you that at least half of them really came to see a display of quite a different kind.

Fed up with hand-swinging, the military next invested in cartridge starters for its piston engines. In these, a set of quite large black-powder cartridges is loaded into a breech magazine attached to the engine. One cartridge, one start. As with the hand-swinging method, success depends on having the cylinders correctly primed with fuel and air and the plugs producing a healthy spark. It has not been unknown for a whole set of cartridges to be fired without success and for the aircraft to sit there, red-hot and untouchable, until everything has cooled down.

Eventually electric starters came on the scene, but these require the aircraft to carry a battery big enough (and therefore heavy) to power them. And if you have to 'flog' the starter to get the engine going, the subsequent high re-charging current stands a good chance of boiling the battery at just about the time the aircraft takes off. To an experienced pilot, a smell of bad eggs on climb-out in an aeroplane means a lapse in behaviour of neither freight nor passengers; it means a boiling battery.

Jet engines brought with them a whole new set of starting problems. You cannot hand-crank a jet engine because your hands won't go round fast enough. You cannot swing it because you would get your fingers caught in the blades if you tried. Even if that was possible, you couldn't spin it fast enough. You can spin it up with a cartridge (Hunter, Canberra, boom-whoosh, big plume of black cordite smoke), with AVPIN (Belvedere, Javelin, Lightning), with a source of compressed air (Trident) or with an electric motor (Comet), but then the fun really starts.

Jet engines perform as advertised when compressed air (supplied from the compressor, in the front) mixes with sprayed fuel in a combustion chamber and the resulting hot gas stream goes through a turbine (which is there to drive the front compressor) and discharges as a jet from the pipe out the back. To control a jet engine you control the flow of fuel to the burners in the combustion chamber. When jet engines are running they are simple and very efficient. Getting them running is, however, entirely another matter and early jet operators must have wondered why nature had not provided them with four pairs of eyes and five pairs of hands.

Let us sit on a flight deck and attempt to start an engine on an early jet airliner. First, you have to get fuel to the engine by turning on low-pressure fuel pumps in the tanks and by opening the low-pressure fuel cocks to the engine. This gets fuel as far as the engine-driven high pressure fuel pump where it is ready to spring into action at your wise command. But not yet, because the next stage is spinning up that compressor. Let's assume we have a diesel-electric trolley screaming under the wing, and a friendly starter crew. The diesel-electric trolley simply supplies the electrical power we need for the starter motor, but the starter crew is there for three very important reasons: to ensure that there is no one behind you, to keep a sharp look-out for signs of fire, and to operate the fire extinguisher if the second reason goes positive and they see anything exciting.

If you are lucky and organised, the starter crew have a headset and you can talk to them, but if not, you signal your readiness to start by spinning your index finger around where the starter crew can see it. If all is clear behind, they respond with the same sign and a thumbs-up. You push the start button and the large electric motor attached to the engine spins up the compressor. You monitor the compressor RPM gauge with one pair of eyes, while keeping an eye on the starter crew with another. When the compressor RPM reaches a level where the maker's manual alleges that the engine is capable of self-sustained operation, you simultaneously hold down the igniter switch with one hand (and you may even hear the 'crack, crack, crack' of the ignition system from the flight deck) while opening the engine high-pressure (HP) fuel cock with another. With your third pair of eyes you make sure that fuel is flowing to the engine and with your fourth you monitor the inlet temperature to the turbine. As the fuel/air stream ignites, the turbine temperature will suddenly leap from twenty degrees to many hundreds Centigrade and the compressor RPM (remember your first pair of eyes?) should start to build too. If the engine has lit promptly, the turbine temperature should climb to a level that is just under the permitted maximum. If it overshoots the normal level and rapidly approaches the maximum, you have less than half a second in which to make your decision to shut off the fuel supply by closing the HP cock and hence shut the engine down. Delay longer and the turbine will melt. And don't forget to keep an eye on the starter crew! They are your eyes on the engine and around the aircraft where you cannot see.

Get it wrong another way, by opening the HP fuel cock and starting the igniters early when the compressor is turning too slowly, and you will deposit a large quantity of unburned fuel in the jet pipe where it will catch fire spectacularly when the main burner does eventually ignite. This is a 'wet start' and looks much worse than it is, but it cooks the jet pipe with a roaring howl and for some reason this can make you unpopular with the maintenance people. Do it at night for best effect. All sorts of people get interested in thirty feet of kerosene flame shooting out of the back of a jet engine. Passengers love it.

And there you are! If you were slick on the fuel cocks, if you held down the igniter button properly, if the instruments were all reading accurately so that the decisions you made were indeed correct and timely, you will have a sweetly running jet engine with RPMs, temperatures and pressures that make sense and give you some sort of confidence that all will continue to be well when you demand much more of the engine in about twenty minutes time. Now, you have three more engines on which to perform the same, exact trick...

Happily, technology has moved on from those early days of manually nurtured starts in Boeing 707s, Comets and the like. The Boeing 747-400 and other modern types have a start button and all the rest of the start sequence is automatic. Even the source of starting energy is on board, in the shape of compressed air from the auxiliary power unit, the APU, which is a tiny gas turbine (usually in the tail) and is small enough to be started by the aircraft's own battery. With modern starting systems, if the computer that monitors temperatures and pressures doesn't like what it senses, the engine will be shut down in an instant and a full diagnosis will be extractable from the on-board systems. Magic.

In the past, however, it has sometimes been necessary to start engines using magic of a different kind. During the Borneo conflict in the early 1960s, RAF Whirlwind 10 helicopters were used for a variety of support and re-supply tasks in the deep jungle territory on the island. There was only one problem with the Whirlwind 10, which was powered by a single Bristol-Siddeley Gnome gas turbine engine: it wouldn't always start.

The reason was nothing to do with the engine or its starter, which was an electric motor that was quite capable of spinning up the engine when powered by the aircraft's batteries. The problem was the igniter plugs, set in the combustion chamber of the tiny engine, because they often failed after giving only a few starts. All Whirlwind crewmen carried a spare igniter plug in their flying overalls when there were any to be had. Unhappily, there were usually none to be had when you really needed one. In extremis, you could usually achieve one start from a failed plug by removing the plug and scribing the insulator between the electrodes with a 2B lead pencil, then replacing the plug. Just one start, in extremis. You could recognise a Whirlwind crewman coming the other way at a glance; he would be carrying a 2B lead pencil in the sleeve pocket of his flying suit.

One day up-country in Borneo a Whirlwind was positioned on a hill-top rendezvous, quite close to the Indonesian border, where some forces had been involved in an internal security operation in the jungle below. At the appointed time the patrol were heard coming up the hill and from the noise it was apparent that they were being pursued. As they appeared, the pilot started the compressor, opened the HP cock and pressed the igniter switch as they tumbled into the cabin. No start. The crewman had no spare igniter plug because there were absolutely none to be had. Presumably someone in the supply chain had decided there was no call for them in Far East Air Force that month. But the crewman had his trusty 2B pencil. He jumped out, raised the panel next to the engine, quickly removed the igniter plug and gave it the 2B pencil treatment. The noise of the pursuers got louder and understandably the troops in the cabin, who had no ambitions to meet them again in a social setting, became somewhat agitated. With the igniter plug replaced and the panel lowered, the crewman signalled to the pilot to start again. Disaster. A 'wheee' from the compressor, but no 'crack, crack' from the igniter. The last option, gone! The noise from the pursuers got even louder. The crewman ran to the cabin and tried the only option he could think of. He grabbed an empty milk bottle and dived under the aircraft to fill it with kerosene from the water-check drain cock underneath the fuselage. Fortunately there was no water, only fuel in the bottle when he had finished. He then soaked a rag in the fuel and opened the nose 'bonnet' of the Whirlwind to expose the engine intake. The pilot realised what he was trying to do and ran up the engine compressor yet again on the battery. The crewman lit the fuel soaked rag, placed it around the vane in the intake and poured raw fuel over it and past it so that the flaming fuel passed into the compressor. As the pilot saw the temperature gauge lift he opened the HP cock and the engine lit! As the rotors started to turn the crewman pulled the rag away and threw it on the ground, closed the bonnet and ran. He was hauled by the patrol into the cabin as the helicopter lifted off, just as the enemy pursuers appeared at the edge of the clearing. Even when the 2B pencil fails, they have ways....

I tell the tale as a tribute to all helicopter crewmen and flight engineers, often (as they are) up against it and many miles from home and help. The aviation world is peppered with them. Not for them only slavish obedience to the rulebook and hence automatic defeat when faced with an unprecedented problem. Their rulebook is for guidance only because they have to deal with unique situations. For them, think imagination, creativity, versatility, wit and wisdom, the quest for total triumph in the face of difficulty, and all the while never expecting anybody to fly in an aircraft they weren't about to fly in themselves. Surely the ultimate example of putting one's money where one's mouth is.

Even when you succeed in starting an aircraft the conventional way, things can still go spectacularly wrong, especially when someone involved is lacking the experience to handle an unusual situation. In the mid-1970s the RAF experimented for a time with a low-cost way of running aircraft operations: Flight Line Mechanics. These airmen and airwomen were trained just to re-fuel aircraft, replenish oils, change tyres and brake parachutes etc., and to act as a starter crew with a fire extinguisher when sending an aircraft on its way. They had little other engineering training and consequently few other skills. Most important, because of their narrow training they lacked 'airmanship', that deep appreciation of all the factors associated with safe flying. One definition of airmanship is "exercising your superior judgement so that you or some other poor soul doesn't have to exercise his superior skill." Lacking a breadth of skills, flight line mechanics had to sit around idle, at least in engineering terms, when flying stopped for any reason. Their morale on one squadron was not helped by a slogan that appeared one morning over their crew-room door, courtesy of their airframe and engine-fitter colleagues in the hangar: 'Give us the job and we'll finish the tools'.

Late one winter afternoon in 1975, just as it was getting dark, two flight line mechanics acted as starter crew for an RAF Lightning being launched on a post engine-change air test. After the pilot had started the engines and closed his cockpit hood, one airman removed the ladder and the chock in front of the port tyre, but then took an unwise short cut, running under the nose of the aircraft to remove the other chock. As he passed under the nose, the powerful vortex coming out of the air intake from the running engines sucked him off the ground and lifted him up half into the intake. The pilot could see nothing of this. The mechanic kicked and struggled and broke free, picked himself up from the tarmac and ran away. His colleague, who was standing fifty feet in front of the aircraft to marshal it out, stood transfixed at the spectacle and then, when it was apparently over, simply thought "gosh, that was lucky" and carried on regardless. He signalled to the pilot (who was still unaware of the whole thing) to taxi, and off the aircraft went. The two mechanics collected themselves and went across to the warm line hut to tell their story. The Chief Technician in charge of the line listened and looked them up and down. "What happened to your pocket?" he asked the unfortunate airman. The whole pocket of the airman's cold weather parka had disappeared.

"It must have been sucked into the aircraft, Chief."

"And what was in the pocket, son?"

"A torch and a screwdriver, Chief."

By this time the aircraft was airborne and Flight Lieutenant Keith Hartley (later a Eurofighter development test pilot with BAE Systems) was in a smooth, accurate climb and taking meticulous altitude, time and engine power readings. Quickly the squadron operations radioed him to bring the aircraft back. Flight Lieutenant Hartley was reluctant: "nothing wrong with this aircraft, two good engines here - the Ts and Ps (temperatures and pressures) are perfect". But of course good airmanship at last prevailed and he returned high in the overhead to burn fuel down to maximum landing weight before landing. As the aircraft taxied in, in total darkness by now, but with the arc-lamps of the base burning all around, the engineering officer could just make out the familiar grin in the cockpit and could read the thinks bubble emanating from under the bone dome: "damned engineers, always panicking over nothing". As Flight Lieutenant Hartley stop-cocked the No. 1 engine, a huge grinding noise occurred and sparks flew out of the back end, accompanied by large pieces of engine. When the upper No. 2 was shut down, even bigger bangs happened and even larger pieces of metal appeared, tinkling across the concrete as they came to rest. Both engines had suffered major damage from foreign object ingestion. But neither engine had complained in flight at high power settings and both had been under the close scrutiny of an experienced flight test pilot. The Rolls-Royce Avon 302 in the Lightning could take a lot of punishment. In the RAF, Flight Line Mechanics did not have to take their punishment for long; a few years later the trade was abolished and the keen ones got the proper training as airframe and engine fitters that they had so long deserved. Starting aeroplanes, indeed any involvement with aircraft is, like flying them, a serious business, not simple and not to be taken lightly.

10

Things on Wings and Things

Having got the mighty machine started, the next logical thing to do is to go flying in it. But before that, has it ever occurred to you why aircraft are the way they are? What is it exactly that decrees that an airliner, for example, should be a long, shiny aluminium tube with various bits attached to it and sticking out of it? Is it just that the designer saw another one and thought "no point in straining myself, I'll design mine like that, too", or is there some more subtle reason? In fact there are thousands of reasons, all of them subtle, and many of them learned the hard way.

Let's start with the load-carrying part, called the fuselage. The requirement is for a space big enough to accommodate a certain number of people, say 200, together with their bags, in enough comfort to enable them to travel for three to four hours – UK to the Canary Islands, or New York to Florida. How best to do that? Well, transporting any solid object through the air incurs drag, as we saw in Chapter 3. Minimise the drag and you will also minimise the fuel you need to burn on the journey, thus making it as cheap as possible, and you will also maximise the speed with which this object can be propelled through the air. What is the shape that has minimum drag and therefore meets these requirements? It turns out to be a cylinder, long thin and streamlined, that travels end-on to the air. So it is not surprising that most aircraft fuselages are long, thin cylinders. They don't have to be; some aircraft like the Shorts 360 have square section fuselages, designed for ease of manufacture (lots of flat metal skin as opposed to all-curved, which is expensive), and also designed to maximise the load they can carry, rather than for minimum drag. To the industry, however, the Shorts 360 is affectionately known as 'The Shed'. Some people say it flies like one too.

Whether tube-like or shed-like, the load-carrying fuselage has to be coaxed off the ground if it is to fly. Not many fuselages can be made the right shape to develop enough lift to support themselves – the Space Shuttle is perhaps the closest example and that is not designed to climb or fly continuously in the air, only to glide and descend to land. To climb and cruise, an aircraft needs wings to provide the necessary lift and, as we saw in Chapter 3, these have to be attached somewhere on the fuselage close to the centre of gravity of the whole aircraft. Should they be attached to the top or bottom of the fuselage? Here the design engineer has some choice. With wings attached to the top, all the passengers get a splendid view of the ground out of the windows in flight. What is more, refuelling and replenishment vehicles can get under the wing while the aircraft is on the ground and passengers can step out just a few feet down aircraft stairs on to the tarmac. But the main undercarriage legs, which are always a weighty item, may have to be particularly long and heavy if they are housed in a high-mounted wing. Most airliners have low-mounted wings because the total structure weight tends to be lowest that way.

*"... there are a number of areas of design where
the engineer has a great deal of discretion..."*

How big must the wings be? Given an efficient wing design, with so many pounds of lift available per square foot, you just need a wing of sufficient square footage to lift the loaded fuselage, surely? But wait a minute, those wings weigh something, too. So you also need more wing area to lift the weight of that first amount of wing, then there is fuel that must be lifted, not to mention the weight of the engines, all of which means a still bigger wing, which itself of course has weight that has to be lifted, and so on! Then there are the tail and vertical fin surfaces at the back of the aircraft (necessary for stability as we saw in Chapter 3), all of which also have weight and have to be lifted. You can see that the design engineer has something of a circular problem. If he or she gets it wrong and the wing isn't big enough for the whole job, the aircraft will not fly, at least not without going very fast to take off. Hence the joke about the early jets that went along the lines 'the only thing that gets that aircraft airborne is the curvature of the earth'. But if the design engineer makes the wing too big, it will be too heavy and contribute too much drag. Then the aircraft will be inefficient because it can carry fewer passengers and will burn more fuel countering the extra drag. It will not sell well (if at all) when its competitors do the job so much better.

After that argument you probably wonder why all aircraft don't look exactly the same, whoever makes them. To some people, doubtless they do. In fact, there are a number of areas of design where the engineer has a great deal of discretion. For example, should he or she hang the engines under the wings, like on the big Boeings and on the various Airbus models? Or should the engines be fixed to the rear of the fuselage, like on the Vickers VC-10, the BAC One-Eleven, the McDonnell-Douglas MD-80 or the Fokker 100? 'Engines hanging on the wings' wins the argument if numbers of aircraft built are anything to go by and there are both obvious and not-so-obvious reasons for this. Engines that sit close to the ground offer easiest access for servicing, or for engine changes. But there is a more subtle reason for the designer to have chosen this way of mounting the engines: the overall structural weight of the aircraft is lower if aircraft are designed that way. You remember that the wing had to lift the fuselage, the fuel, the engines, and its own weight? Well, if the fuel and the engines were all inside the fuselage or attached to it, the wing root, that is the thick piece of wing structure where the wing joins the fuselage, would have to be big and beefy to lift the whole load. Putting engines and fuel on and in the wings saves you lots of structural weight at the wing root, as this example explains. Imagine you were a mouse, walking from the tip of a Boeing 747 wing, past the hanging engines towards the fuselage. As you walked you would have passed a greater and greater wing area that had provided lift to the aircraft. As you stepped over the point where an engine was attached to the wing, you would realise that the wing area ahead of you, as you approached the fuselage, now had one less engine to carry. Go past the next engine on your way to the fuselage and you have another engine that the wing has 'carried already' and that the wing root ahead of you does not need to concern itself about. This is why the wing roots of aircraft like the Boeings and the Airbuses are thinner and lighter than those on the VC-10, MD-80 and the like – the engines have been 'carried already' by the wing. Hanging the engines on the wings gives a lower overall structure weight for the aircraft, and lower structure weight gives you the ability to put more revenue-earning load, passengers or freight, into the aircraft. A higher payload gives better operating economics for the aircraft type and that sells airliners.

So why would anyone do it differently? Why did the VC-10 etc. get designed the way they did? There are many reasons and the first stems from some of the disadvantages of engines hanging from the wings. First and foremost is that the presence of the engine and its support breaks up the airflow over what would otherwise be a smooth wing. Slats, the high-lift devices on the leading edge of the wing, and flaps, the high lift devices that trail from the wing, both have to be split and have sections missing when the engines are mounted on the wing. When the Vickers VC-10 was being designed, a vital part of BOAC's performance specification was an acceptable take-off performance from their hot and high African destinations such as Nairobi. A full-span clean wing was the only answer with the jet engines of the day and so the VC-10 was designed with a clean big-lifting wing with full-span slats and flaps, and its engines were placed at the back of the fuselage. But the wing was heavier as a result, and putting the engines at the back meant that the horizontal tail had to be put on top of the vertical stabiliser or fin, which meant that the fin had to carry all the loads from the tail down to the fuselage, making it also beefier and heavier than a normal fin of that size.

But fuselage-mounted engines on an aircraft have another advantage and this relates to the ability of the aircraft to land in cross-winds. A large aircraft approaching to land in a cross-wind needs to fly 'wing-low' towards the side wind so as not to drift off the centreline of the runway. Flying this way, engines hanging low under the wing could strike the runway before the main undercarriage. So an aircraft type such as a small Airbus with wing-mounted engines might be more limited operationally in crosswinds than an MD-80 or a BAC One-Eleven and might have to divert when one of those latter two could have landed.

Another disadvantage of the wing-mounted engine design comes about when you consider the possibility of an engine failure. If an outer engine fails on a wing-mounted engine design like a Boeing 747, the 'good' engine that mirrors it on the other wing still produces thrust and so gives the aircraft a large yawing or sideways-turning force towards the dead engine. This needs a large force from the rudder to counteract. Large rudder forces, especially if they are to be available at low speeds such as during take-off, mean that the aircraft needs a large rudder and hence a large vertical stabiliser or fin. These weigh more and have more drag in normal flight, both factors that eat into the advantage that wing-mounted engine designs have over rear-mounted ones.

So you see, it is not a simple decision. It is made even more complicated by another, unpredictable factor: passenger preference. The rear-mounted engines on the VC-10 made its cabin quieter than that of the Boeing 707 that was its contemporary. It turned out that passengers preferred the VC-10, given a choice, and BOAC's VC-10s throughout the 1960s enjoyed much higher load factors than did competitors' Boeings on the same routes. On paper the VC-10 was less economical to operate than the 707, but flying 80% full of passengers rather than 65% made the revenue and net profit figures tell a different story. It was the simple, paper argument, however, that caused

BOAC to announce in 1968 that it would abandon the VC-10 as a long-term prospect. Doubtless its management assumed that the airline's service was so special that it could achieve 80% passenger load factors on an all-Boeing fleet as well.

Passenger appeal, or the opposite, is an important factor in aircraft design. When the Vickers VC-10 was being designed at Weybridge, someone had the idea of putting the flight deck, with the aircrew, up in the tail bullet at the top of the fin. It makes sense to place it up there, because the control runs to the engines, tail surfaces and rudders would be the shortest possible, saving a lot of weight. Moreover, the nose of the aircraft could be made into a lounge with the most fantastic views for the first-class passengers, especially of take-off and landing. Market research, alas, showed that this would not be a popular idea, as passengers preferred the illusion that they were somehow safer when the pilots were ahead of them rather than behind them. It may be that first-class passengers in the nose of a Boeing 747 have not realised to this day that their captain and co-pilot are, in fact, some way above them and behind them. Look at a Boeing 747 next time you are at an airport and you'll see what I mean.

In an aircraft design, weight is so critical that everything is there for a reason – or it wouldn't be there at all because a 'nice-to-have' would have been deleted at a design review long before. So it can be an entertaining exercise to look at an airliner, parked outside a departure lounge in the minutes before you are asked to climb into it and ask yourself on observing some feature "why on earth did they do that?" For example, next time you leave for home from a small holiday airport and stand at the foot of the steps at the front of an MD-80, Fokker 100 or similar rear-engine type, look at the nose-wheel tyres. There is a rubber ridge or chine moulded into one sidewall, the outer sidewall, on both sides. Why? Why would they do that? A chined tyre is heavier than a plain tyre, almost certainly more expensive, and the tyre can only be fitted to a nose-wheel one way. Why would they go to that complexity and expense and, what is more, introduce the potential for a Murphy? The answer is simple: when the first rear-engined jet airliner, the French Sud-Aviation Caravelle, was test-flown, the first one to take off from a wet runway threw so much water and spray up into the engines from the nose-wheels that the engines flamed out – the water put out the fire. The engines stopped and, if the runway had been shorter, the aircraft would have run off the end at high speed. So those rubber chines on the outer part of the nose-wheels are, in fact, carefully designed water and spray deflectors that make that particular type of aircraft safe to operate in the wet. For those, you can thank the team at the Kleber Tyre Company in France who solved what was a real show-stopper of a problem. They did it simply, reliably and cheaply, and in a way that could be used on all subsequent aircraft types that might suffer from the same problem.

Other efforts to achieve reliability and cheapness of aircraft operations have centred around the manufacturing process. The British aircraft industry and airlines in the 1960s and 1970s were clearly upset by the apparent injustice of the dominance of the American companies in airliner manufacture. 'Ours are better!' was the honest and frustrated cry. "When you step into the doorway of a Boeing airliner," a British aircraft manufacturer told a gathering of students, "look down the fuselage at the line of rivets.

... everything is there for a reason...

They're all over the place! On one of ours, they're in a perfect straight line." The students did look and the man from British Aircraft Corporation was right. But his aircraft cost X to build and more to buy, and Boeings cost Y and their sale price was lower. Crucially, Boeings were just as durable in service as their British rivals and cheaper and simpler to repair. One British Airways hangar superintendent said, "I hated the Boeings at first. But once I understood the philosophy of how they had been designed and built, and saw that they were perfectly safe, just different, I was converted. They were much easier to work on."

British aircraft were well made, almost over-engineered. For the VC-10 and the One-Eleven in the 1960s, Vickers and the British Aircraft Corporation went to great lengths and expense to achieve a near identical standard of airframe component production. Wing planks, for example, were cut using the latest numerically controlled cutting machines so that all wing planks were interchangeable. 'Interchangeability' was the proud watchword on the VC-10 production line at Brooklands, Weybridge. So much so that it jarred a little to one university vacation student, working in the final assembly building in the summer of 1963, when he saw two fitters struggling to fit a passenger door to G-ARVJ that they had 'robbed' from G-ARVK. It didn't fit and the lack of door was holding up G-ARVJ's pre-first-flight pressurisation tests. The undergraduate, in all innocence, sought the counsel of Bert Lambert, the final assembly shop supervisor, who cut a dashing figure in his snow white boiler suit. Bert had worked at Vickers since he left school and was shortly to retire. As an apprentice he had helped build the Vimy bomber in which Alcock and Brown had first crossed the Atlantic in 1919; there wasn't much about aeroplanes that Bert didn't know.

"Mr Lambert, I don't understand," said the student. "…if all the parts on the VC-10 are interchangeable, why won't Victor Kilo's door fit on Victor Juliet? They've been struggling for hours."

"Son," said Bert, putting a grandfatherly arm around the student's shoulder. "Just between you and me, the only thing that's interchangeable on this aircraft is the air in the tyres."

The student remembered this wisdom throughout his subsequent career in aircraft maintenance engineering and reckons that it stood him in excellent stead.

Sitting in an airliner and looking out at the wing as the aircraft prepares for take-off makes you realise that there is a lot more to a wing than just a simple metal structure containing fuel. There are many fixed and moving parts on a wing, a real assortment of flaps and slats, all designed for important purposes. On taxying out before take-off, you get the first indication that something important is happening to the wing when you hear a whirring noise under your feet. A motor is powering one of the wing parts and you can see movement on the wing out of the window. Out of its front edge 'grow' the slats, as if by some mechanical magic, as the leading edge of the wing moves forward and down. Simultaneously, the flaps at the trailing edge move out a bit, powered by large hydraulic spiral jacks (flapjacks!), and also move down. The effects of both these wing surface movements are first to make the whole wing bigger, and second to make it more curved, fore and aft. This greater area and curvature, or 'camber', enable the wing to produce more lift without having to go fast so it can support the aircraft's heavy take-off weight at the required low take-off speed.

Once airborne, with the aircraft climbing away and accelerating, both the slats and the flaps go in, bit by bit, until the wing is 'clean'. The rumbling vibration from the airflow goes, as if by magic. You can think of air as aerodynamicists do: air is fussy, it loves a clean wing and shows its disapproval when confronted with anything less. At the lower airspeeds at take-off and in the climb, the low-speed ailerons, hinged surfaces at the trailing edge of the outer wings near the wing-tip, move to keep the aircraft level or turn it at the pilot's command. Just as on the simple gliders of Chapter 5, as the aileron surface goes up, lift is shed and the wing goes down. On the other wing the opposite is always happening with the other aileron. But, as speed builds, these large outer ailerons on the outer wings of some high speed jet aircraft can become too sensitive and effective and sometimes their job is taken over by a much smaller inboard set. If you are in a window seat near the trailing edge of the wing, look for an inner set of smaller, high-speed ailerons. See how slightly they have to move to get the aircraft to roll into a turn.

Why is the end of the wing turned up on some aircraft? Those so-called 'winglets' at the tips of the wings cut the drag of the wing and so improve the aircraft's fuel consumption and range. They were invented by Richard Whitcomb, an aerodynamic genius who worked for NASA in the 1960s and who saw this clever way to reduce drag. In Chapter 3 you will recall that the lift on the wing was produced by a combination of higher air pressure underneath the wing and lower air pressure on the upper surface. Unfortunately the presence of those two different pressures means that, at the wing tip, the higher pressure air under the wing tries to flow round the tip to the lower pressure area on top. This swirling action creates a trailing vortex from the wing tip, a swirling trailing funnel of air, and this produces drag. Whitcomb's winglets provide an obstacle to that flow. They act as a simple barrier to the span-wise flow around the wing tip, reduce the strength of the trailing vortex and hence reduce the drag. With clever design they also act rather like the sail of a boat when it is close-hauled into wind by developing a forward thrust force that further reduces the net drag. Their exact effect can be quantified because the winglets on the Airbus 320 are removable, for maintenance reasons, and the aircraft is perfectly flyable without them. Without them, however, an Airbus burns 1.5 percent more fuel in the cruise, nearly forty pounds weight of kerosene during each hour of flight.

What are those little bits of angled metal seemingly glued to the top surface of the outer wing? Remember the unassailable logic: they are on the aircraft, they weigh something, they must therefore have a purpose. They are vortex generators - they each create a vortex, a little spinning wake of air that bites on the control surface behind. Although vortices create drag, these are necessary in this position, just forward of the hinged control surface. Without them, the air would just skate smoothly over the top of the control surface and fine adjustments of the controls would have no effect.

And those wick-like things at the wing-tip, trailing in the airflow? Those are static electricity dischargers, designed to earth the aircraft as it flies along. If the aircraft builds up a static charge by flying through cloud, it will shed it into the air through the fibres of those wicks. There are no prizes for touching one on the ground, however. Even though the rubber tyres conduct build-ups of static electricity to the ground, ever since Dunlop developed the electrically conducting aircraft tyre during the 1940s, the static wicks can still carry a substantial charge just after an aircraft lands and will deliver a nasty shock. Some have experienced it and have not lived to tell the tale.

In the descent, the pilot may be told to lose a lot of height quickly, to take advantage of some opportunity spotted by air traffic control. On the top surface of each wing, hinged flat plates called 'lift-dumpers' or 'spoilers', extend by means of hydraulic rams to 'spoil' the airflow on the top of the wing, where most of the lift comes from. The aircraft descends rapidly and when the target height is reached, in go the spoilers and the cobblestone rumble they cause disappears with them. An unpopular RAF officer deservedly acquired the nickname 'Lift-dumper'. He had a tendency to pop up and spoil things.

The overall 'handling' characteristics of the airliner, the ease with which it can be flown, are the results of a painstaking programme of flight testing the prototype aircraft. The aircraft that goes into service may look the same as the prototype that flew years ago, but at the controls it will usually be a very different aeroplane. During the flying development programme, the manufacturer's test pilots set about creating an aircraft that can be operated confidently and safely by airline pilots of varying experience, all of whom at some stage will be new to the aircraft type. The company test pilots will identify many necessary modifications to the type's flying characteristics and these changes will be incorporated into all production aircraft before the aircraft type is finally assessed by the CAA's test pilots and granted its Certificate of Airworthiness. Only then can it go into service and carry passengers. Test pilots can be quite tart in their observations. When evaluating a new type of aircraft in the military support role, one test pilot included in his report the following criticism: "Access to the cockpit is difficult." Then he added as an afterthought, with the whole flying assessment and the future safety of his fellow aircrew in mind: "It should be made impossible."

Ten miles from landing, take-off slat and flap motor out slowly from the leading and trailing edges of the wing, to increase its lifting ability so that it can support the aircraft at the lower speed at which it must now fly. Closer to the airport more flap is extended, enabling the aircraft to fly as slow as 160 knots, then full flap is selected just before landing. Although the aircraft is flying more slowly than at any previous time, the engine note increases as power is applied to overcome the extra drag of the flaps, slats and, by now, the undercarriage that has also been extended.

If your window seat is in the right place, in the final few hundred feet before landing you can often see the ground between the flaps and the supporting spars and structure of the wing. So much of what appeared to be a solid metal wing turns out to be deployable control surfaces. You can feel lots of buffet and rumble from all this extended metalwork, and on a damp day you can sometimes see a cloudy vortex as well. The spinning whirlwind of air shed from the corners of a flap has such a low pressure at its centre that its humidity condenses out into a stream of private cloud behind the aircraft.

As the aircraft touches the runway, the lift-dumpers on the wing's top surface extend suddenly to kill the lift and keep the airliner firmly on the ground. The airborne bit is over, but definitely not the flying. There is still at least one most important and challenging part of the flying operation still to come and it all happens in the next twenty seconds. It is called stopping - and it is not as easy as it sounds.

11

Brake Dancing

Aircraft belong in the air, not on the ground. Once they touch the ground they start to get difficult, no more so when they have just landed and need to stop. A Boeing 747 at average landing weight, arriving on the concrete at 145 knots (167 mph) possesses a lot of energy, energy that can be calculated by multiplying half the mass by the velocity squared. Don't do it - accept my word for it, it's lots. It's enough to kick a double-decker London bus from sea level to the top of Mount Everest, or, closer to home, enough energy to kick eight buses to the top of Mount Snowdon. Energy like that doesn't go anywhere without a bit of help and help at that stage, as an aircraft lands, is in short supply. The energy absorbed by the wheels and tyres beginning to turn as they hit the concrete slows the aircraft down, but not by much. It does decrease it by enough, however, to make it a bad idea to pre-spin the wheels in the air before landing (as some have proposed) in order to lessen the puff of blue smoke on touchdown and so improve tyre life. Doing that would add energy to the whole aircraft and so make even greater total energy to get rid of before the houses at the end of the runway loomed large in the windscreen. So a puff of smoke from the tyres is a good thing, as is making use of the drag from the flaps (hanging down behind and below the wing), the spoilers (poking up from the top of the wing), and the airbrakes (hanging out at the back of the fuselage). They all help a bit, but most of the work is going to be done, at least on an airliner, by reverse thrust from the engines and by the brakes. But reverse thrust is too noisy to use at London Heathrow or at Sydney (to give just two examples) at five o'clock in the morning. And not all airliner types even have reverse thrust - the BAe146/Avro RJ regional jet series, for example. Without doubt it is brakes that do most of the work.

During the braked deceleration down the runway, the brakes turn the motion energy (or to give it its proper name, kinetic energy) of the landing aircraft into heat. And into a bit of noise, perhaps, with a brake squeal or two, but noise doesn't absorb much energy. Brakes mostly produce heat. A great deal of it. If you are ever privileged enough to be out on an airfield at night near the end of the runway, and if the lights aren't too bright, you can see the brake packs glowing red as the landing aircraft turn off the runway and taxi past. The latest carbon brakes reach white heat. That stored heat is dissipated quickly through conduction into the surrounding structure and through convection into the air. There is some radiation too, because you can feel the heat from the brake on your cheek when you go near it. Don't ever touch a brake, not for a very long time after it has been used. If a brake catches fire, you cannot put water or any liquid on it, as rapid cooling and contraction of the components would cause it to explode. Dry powder is the only safe extinguishing agent for brake fires.

Brakes make a very important contribution to safe aircraft operations. The most testing case they are designed for is not in fact that of landing, but a rejected take-off when an aircraft at maximum weight stops from a high speed in the runway length remaining. The aircraft's energy then is twice the typical landing energy - enough to kick *sixteen* buses to the top of Mount Snowdon! As aircraft have become heavier and take-off decision speeds faster, the energy absorption required of the brakes has tested designers' ingenuity to the limits. It isn't just the heat absorption that offers the challenge in wheels and brakes, which of course must be as small in size and weight as possible, it is the dissipation of that heat afterwards that also concentrates the mind. Where is it going to go? Into the tyres? Not a good idea because the fusible safety plugs in the tyres will melt (they are designed to, just before the tyre would burst) and the tyre will deflate leaving the aircraft stranded. No, the heat must be absorbed into the brake pack and then shed safely into the air and into the metal structure of the undercarriage.

While acknowledging the skill of all aircraft brake manufacturers in their ever-sophisticated aircraft brake designs over the years, one man and his team deserve to be singled out for two developments that have added much to the safety of landing aircraft over the past fifty years. These developments were the disc brake and the anti-skid unit, and the leader of the team that developed them was Dunlop's Henry W. Trevaskis. Born in Paris in 1902, the son of a jeweller, Henry came to England in 1919 unable to speak the language. He got a job in Birmingham as a floor sweeper with the Lombard Tyre and Rim Company and, despite his initial language problems, his keen brain soon found him a place in the drawing office. By the time Dunlop took over the firm in 1925, Henry Trevaskis was proving to be something of an inventor. He invented a machine for painting decorative lines on cycle rims, a job that had cost eleven shillings (55p) per hundred and which Henry's machine reduced to a cost of two and a half pence (1p) per hundred. By the time World War Two arrived, Henry was well enough established for his genius to imprint itself on Dunlop's range of equipment for wartime aircraft. Pneumatic gun-firing gear, aircraft windscreen wipers, electrical de-icing mats on wing leading edges, valves for inflatable life-rafts and much else. After the War, Trevaskis and his team were the first to develop disc brakes for aircraft and quickly saw their potential for high performance cars. Experimental Dunlop disc brakes were fitted to the Jaguar cars entered for the Le Mans 24-hour race in 1953 and Jaguar won first, second and fourth places. The birth of the disc brake was, however, not an easy one. During their early development Dunlop's senior management got wind of the work going into this new type of brake and called a halt to it. At that time Dunlop were not in the car brake business, but they did supply components to the big car brake manufacturers and this market might disappear quickly if they suddenly appeared as competitors. No one deliberately sets out to lose a big business with the aim of replacing it with a small one. Undaunted by this little local difficulty the Dunlop research team quietly and unofficially pressed on, just in the name of research, and the Jaguar outing to Le Mans was the first real trial of the new brakes. It turned out to be an 'outing' of a different kind. The morning after Jaguar's success the national press were full of praise for the drivers, for Jaguar - and for Dunlop's new brakes! Henry's boss was Joe Wright, the managing director of Dunlop Rim and Wheel. Poor Joe's telephone just about jumped off his desk that Monday morning - his presence was required, pronto, at Dunlop's head office in London. He was to be flown down to Croydon by Alex Campbell in the company Dove. With a heavy heart, Joe got out of the company car that had met him at Croydon and made his way into Dunlop's corporate headquarters in King Street, St. James'. Sacked? Not a bit of it – he got promoted on to the Dunlop main board! How refreshing to tell a story of a company board that thinks sense, not spite. Their action stamped Dunlop as an innovative company, which of course subsequently attracted all sorts of new talent.

However, good brakes were only part of the safe stopping equation because, as large passenger aircraft and the jet age arrived, it became clear that something would have to be done about an aircraft's tendency to skid off the side of the runway when landing. The Ministry wanted Dunlop to manufacture an American anti-skid device under licence, but Henry was singularly unimpressed when he saw it. He and his team turned their minds to solving the problem in a more elegant way.

Henry Trevaskis, Frank Mortimer and their colleagues came up with the Dunlop Maxaret. 'Maximum arrête - maximum stop' – Henry's first language had been French, remember? This tiny device transformed the safety of everyday aircraft operations by just about eliminating skidding as a hazard. The Maxaret was (and is) small, simple, light and comparatively cheap. Its automotive successor can be seen today on most cars as the ABS system, which enables you to brake as hard as you like without risk of skidding and, just as important which everybody forgets, steer out of trouble at the same time.

A skidding tyre does not slow you as much as one that is in proper stationary contact with the surface, as any road safety film will show. In a car without ABS you can sometimes 'feel' a tyre begin to skid and skilful drivers can practise 'cadence' braking, repeatedly pumping the brake pedal as fast as they can, so that they achieve best possible braking deceleration from the wheel and tyre. In an aircraft this is impossible as you get little or no feedback from the wheels, especially where a multi-wheel undercarriage is concerned. In the 1950s, large important aircraft were coming on the scene with this problem. Both the Avro Vulcan and Handley Page Victor V-bombers had main undercarriages with four wheels on a big trailing alloy forging hinged to the undercarriage leg above. If left to skid, a locked wheel on one of those would give you much reduced braking efficiency, quickly burst the tyre and perhaps even damage the aircraft with flying shards of rubber. Moreover, if a greater number of port undercarriage wheels were locked than starboard ones, the braking effect that side would be less and round to starboard you would swing, in spite of applying all the left rudder in the world, and you would be quickly off the runway and on to the grass. Heavy aircraft and grass do not make for a mutually supportive relationship, as many an air lifting-bag, shovel, pierced steel plank, arc light and tractor have testified over the years.

The Maxaret was entirely mechanical and worked by sensing the sudden slowing of the wheel as it locked up to skid, and by releasing the pressure to the brake on that wheel, then re-applying it, then releasing it as in cadence braking. It would do all that seven times a second. A tiny unit weighing only 4.7lb, the Maxaret consisted of a small casing that ran in contact with the wheel. The casing contained a small flywheel and normally the two rotated together. When the wheel and casing suddenly slowed, however, as the wheel started to lock, the flywheel in the Maxaret over-ran the casing and operated a valve that released the pressure feed to the brake. As the wheel speeded up, it re-applied it. It was very effective. A test pilot at Boscombe Down reported in *Flight* (now *Flight International*) magazine in October 1953 that he had landed a new RAF heavy bomber on a very wet runway, at twelve percent above his maximum permitted landing weight (test pilots do that...). He applied the brakes at 1,200 pounds per square inch each side from 85 knots and, with Dunlop Maxarets, he stopped in 1,200 yards, with unmarked tyres. Earlier, in an identical aircraft not fitted with Maxarets, he had "great difficulty stopping in 1,600 yards, with a brake parachute, and collected two burst tyres!" The new anti-skid system needed no more selling to the RAF. Dunlop proudly estimated that it "increased the length of a 2,000 yard runway by 800 yards". Fifty years later disc brakes and ABS are just two of the many technologies that have found their way from aviation into everyday use in cars and Henry Trevaskis, Frank Mortimer and their team deserve to be remembered for the contributions they made to the safety of both types of transport.

If stopping aircraft is your business, brake parachutes look an attractive proposition, at least at first glance. Brake parachutes first made an appearance in Germany during World War Two and were used to slow down the very fast rocket-powered fighters that were being developed at that time. The principle is simple: touch down on the runway, pull the release, and a huge canopy deploys behind you, slowing you down for nothing. The trouble is, Murphy's Law says that, if they can be released from the aircraft (as they must), they can also fall off. When that happens, your aircraft has to be equipped with brakes big enough to stop the aircraft on its own anyway. So you cannot save on brake weight with a parachute, just brake wear when everything goes right and the parachute works as advertised. Releasing the braking parachute at the end of the runway (hopefully before it has been trailed across the concrete for too far and has become damaged) usually means it blows sideways on to the grass in the crosswind and gets wet and muddy. Or it lands on the runway and blocks it for landing just when someone else is right behind you on a short final approach (Sod's Corollary to Murphy's Law, remember, from Chapter 8). In any event, collecting it, drying it out and repacking it has proved uneconomic for civil transport operations. The Russians' first jet airliner, the Tupolev Tu-104, routinely used a braking parachute and Sud-Aviation in France fitted them to some of their Caravelle twin-engined airliners in the 1950s, but the idea was soon dropped. Only military aircraft and space shuttles have the 'operating cost is not the biggest issue' philosophy that enables them to make use of braking parachutes.

In the 1960s, someone had the idea of making a gravel deceleration strip at the end of runways, rather in the manner of those quite frightening gravel escape lane strips that you sometimes see for out-of-control lorries as you descend a steep hill. An early Lightning prototype and a Canberra bomber were taxied at high speed off the end of the Royal Aircraft Establishment's runway at Farnborough in Hampshire to investigate the concept. The gravel stopped the aircraft successfully, but in flying up from the wheels the gravel hit the underside of the aircraft's wings and wrecked them. They looked as if they were auditioning as playing surfaces for a steel band. A better idea, tried at RAE Bedford using a Comet 3 airliner, was to spray a bed of urea-formaldehyde foam in a carpet beyond the runway as a Soft Ground Arrester System. This successfully slowed the aircraft and it sustained no damage.

Rotary hydraulic arrester gear (the RHAG) was another solution, where the aircraft would drop a hook to catch an arrester cable and the aircraft's kinetic energy would be transformed into a temperature rise of the hydraulic oil in the RHAG damper drum as the cable ran out from the reel. The RAF installed these as emergency arrester systems for combat aircraft, but the Royal Navy preferred the CHAG, the chain arrester gear. In this scheme, the aircraft would pick up a cable that was attached to a length of heavy ship's chain (waste not, want not, the Royal Navy), and the aircraft would lose its energy by accelerating this heavy chain and dragging it along the runway. Care had to be taken here to set out the chain in the correct way because if the aircraft grabbed too heavy a piece of chain too quickly, the force would be too much simply to decelerate the aircraft and would actually pull its back end off.

"Why all the fuss?" you may ask, "why not just have brakes and very long runways and have done with it?" Two problems there: runways are length-limited by things like quarries, reservoirs and Windsor Castle placed in the way, and the problem with brakes is that in certain circumstances you cannot use up to half of them. If you consider an aircraft landing in a crosswind, the wind from the side of the runway blows sideways against the aeroplane. But if you look at an aeroplane in sideways view, you will see that the biggest part of it is at the back, the vertical stabiliser or fin. When the crosswind blows against that, the aircraft tries to weathercock into the wind rather like a weathervane. To keep the aircraft straight, the pilot can use out-of-wind rudder until the speed decays and the rudder loses its bite, but after that all he has to keep the aircraft going straight down the runway is out-of-wind brake. In other words the pilot cannot use much or any brake on the 'into-wind' main-wheel. 'Half the brakes' means 'half the deceleration' and the situation has all the makings, unless everybody is very careful, for an exploration of the cabbage field at the far end of the runway and a picture in tomorrow's paper.

By the late 1950s it became apparent that a good way to get some effective braking was to reverse the thrust of the engines so that they could decelerate the aircraft when required with something like the same effectiveness that they accelerated it on take-off. With jet engines, with their air designed to flow straight through as easily as possible, this posed something of a design challenge. For some years the old propeller-driven airliners had the ability to turn their propeller blades to a fine or 'superfine' pitch and slow the aircraft down. Watching and listening to a Bristol Britannia land, you could hear the 'growl' from the propellers as braking pitch was selected on all four props during the landing run.

In Britain, the first thrust reversers were designed for the Rolls-Royce Avon in 1955. Two of the four Avons fitted to the Comet 4 airliner had reversers, the outer engine in the wing root on each side. On such engines, selecting 'reverse' causes a pair of movable clamshell doors to rotate from their stored position at the side of the jet-pipe into the gas stream. In doing so, they uncover the ducts on the side of the engine, and vanes in those ducts conduct the jet efflux outwards and forwards so that it opposes the aircraft's motion and slows the aircraft down. As the years have passed and new engines have appeared, the design of thrust reversers has become even more subtle and efficient. If you look at a modern Boeing or Airbus with podded engines, during its landing run the whole rear section of the engines' cowling now seems to slide aft as the reverser is engaged, enabling large amounts of jet efflux to be directed outward and forward to decelerate the aircraft. The pilot can select reverse thrust as soon as the aircraft is firmly on the ground and the engines are at 'idle'. Most passengers will notice both the noise that the reverse thrust makes and the deceleration it causes. Notice, however, that full reverse thrust is cancelled at about eighty knots, well before the aircraft slows to its taxying speed. This is because it is unwise to re-ingest hot exhaust gases into the engine intake – the turbulent hot air can cause stressful airflows in the compressor as well as excessive temperatures further back in the engine's turbine.

Do you remember the problem of landing in a crosswind? In a crosswind the aircraft weathercocks into wind so you can only use the 'out-of-wind' brake and that gives you only half the deceleration. Even with reverse thrust available that can be a problem, as it was one night some years ago for a British Airways Trident crew landing at Edinburgh. The Edinburgh runway in those days was short. Plenty long enough for ordinary Trident operations, but with a crosswind, with only half the braking available, the runway length started to get marginal. With the runway wet too, it started to get very marginal. On the night in question it was indeed very wet and the wind was blowing a good Scottish gale straight across the runway. The BA crew were flying a Trident 3, the largest of the Trident series, which was useful that night because the Trident 3 had one very interesting ability that made it ideal for wet and windy Edinburgh landings: it was cleared to use reverse thrust whilst still airborne to begin its deceleration in the air before its wheels even touched the runway. Given the conditions that night at Edinburgh, the captain checked his performance manual and briefed his crew for just such a landing. When he called for it, just before the aircraft touched down, he briefed the crew that he wanted reverse thrust to be selected on engines one and three so that the aircraft would stop as quickly as it could.

The captain flew a perfect approach, arriving over the runway threshold in just the right attitude and at just the right speed. He called "Reverse!" at the designated point, the co-pilot promptly gave it to him, and once the aircraft was firmly down the captain kept the Trident straight using out-of-wind rudder, calling for reverse thrust to be cancelled as the speed decayed and continuing the deceleration with largely out-of-wind brake. The aircraft slowed quickly, exactly in accordance with their calculations, stopped well before the end of the short runway, and turned off down the taxiway to park at the terminal. Just another sector in Europe's challenging flying conditions, flown by a thoroughly professional crew.

As the passengers were leaving from the forward door, the flight crew emerged through the cockpit door. The captain was intercepted by a little old lady, one of the last passengers to leave. She was a sweet little thing, complete with hat and hatpin.

"Excuse me, Captain," she said, "but I think I know what you did wrong."

The co-pilot and third pilot looked on, beaming.

"Oh really, madam," said the captain, "and what was that?"

"Well," she said, "I have flown in Tridents a lot and when they land they go 'bang, whoosh'. Yours went 'whoosh, bang'."

"Thank you, madam," said the captain. "I'll try to remember that."

Guess who bought the aircrew coffees in the Edinburgh terminal that evening before the last flight back to London Heathrow.

"Watch the flocking birdies, Nigel!"

12

Birds are bad for you

To most ears, 'birds are bad for you' sounds like a piece of fatherly advice that might be dispensed in some soap opera set in the East End of London. To aviation ears, however, the phrase has a telling ring of truth. Most pilots on hearing the phrase will instantly recall a sudden thump during their flying life as one of our feathered friends ran into a wing, a fuselage, an engine intake or even a cockpit window. Birds and aircraft don't mix terribly well because aircraft go so fast they cannot get out of each other's way. Birds, it must be admitted in all fairness, got there first. Their union must be up in arms about the fact that, only in the past hundred years (two milliseconds to midnight in evolutionary terms), some new kid on the block in the shape of the aviator has been demanding rambling rights in their territory. In the early days of the conflict between bird and aeroplane the honours were nearly even, but now it seems the aircraft always wins and the poor bird always comes off worst. That said, no aviator wants even to engage in such a battle, let alone win. If birds can be dissuaded from encountering aeroplanes at high speed, so much the better for everyone. But as far as an aircraft is concerned, a bird is only one kind of hazard. It is no different from anything else solid that does not belong near or in an aircraft, and in the aviation world they are collectively called foreign objects and they cause Foreign Object Damage, known as FOD.

The torch and screwdriver ingested by the RAF Lightning's engines, as recounted in Chapter 9, caused FOD. With an engine disintegrating spectacularly like that, the FOD is not hard to miss. But sometimes the damage to an aircraft or engine is slight, a nick in a compressor blade for example, and its cause is not so obvious so it is blamed on 'a piece of FOD'. Thus in the slightly ungrammatical (but very communicative) world of the aircraft operator, 'FOD' has become the noun describing the cause of the damage as well as the word for the damage itself, not forgetting of course the verb 'to FOD' and the adjective 'FODDED'. FOD is a multi-purpose word and it is just as well that we get our money's worth out of it because it is so expensive. A tiny nick discovered in a compressor blade, although it might appear insignificant, must still be dealt with urgently. If it is not smoothed out (or the blade replaced if the damage is beyond limits and smoothing it out is not possible), the nick will cause the compressor blade to suffer a growing fatigue crack and to break off very soon afterwards, disappearing into the engine and causing much worse FOD, perhaps even engine failure. No future in that.

Aircraft operators take great care to keep pieces of FOD – nuts, bolts, loose articles, locking wire, stones or loose pieces of concrete, for example - off runways and hard-standings where they might get sucked into jet engines or thrown up against an airframe and cause damage. Airfield vehicles can be fitted with special tyres that have smooth treads designed specifically to avoid picking up and spreading FOD. In the RAF sharp-eyed teams of aircraft operators keep airfield surfaces clear of FOD by means of weekly, sometimes daily, sweeps and inspections. The latter process, a slow walk staring at the ground forensic-policeman style in a long line, is always referred to as a 'FOD Plod'. Invitations are extended to other people on the base to join in, then perhaps to a squadron Friday-night shindig afterwards. It is of course every RAF squadron's aim to enlist the help of one or more of the base's security staff in the effort, the Ministry of Defence Police, whereupon it can be truly (but very quietly) called a 'MoD Plod FOD Plod'. Through such occasional triumphs is life made bearable.

The exact way that a jet engine can suck debris (or even a passing flight line mechanic, see Chapter 9) off the ground into an intake was something of a mystery for a while. At the Proof Experimental Establishment at Shoeburyness an old Lightning fighter (ex-RAE Bedford) was pressed into service to try to discover more. Inviting-looking FOD, in the shape of polystyrene granules on a tray, were placed under the intake with the engines running to investigate the areas from which they would be sucked into the intake. They weren't! They stayed resolutely put. And yet in certain conditions, with a crosswind blowing sideways across the engine air intake perhaps, a vortex would suddenly form and emerge from the intake like a mini-tornado and anything this spinning tube touched would be sucked up: polystyrene granules, the tray holding them, anybody careless enough still to be holding the tray, etc., etc. Occasionally at an airport on a damp humid day, out of the window at the departure gate you will see a nearby aircraft start up and a white tube will appear to grow out of the engine and touch the ground. This vortex, made visible by the water vapour condensing out in its low pressure core just like a full-scale tornado, will suck into the engine anything it comes into contact with. It was one of these that lifted the poor flight line mechanic into the Lightning's intake and ate his pocket, complete with torch and screwdriver. As long as the aircraft parking stand is FOD-free and mechanic-free, the most that will usually get sucked into the engine is a puddle of standing water that does no harm at all, but the effect is quite dramatic to watch.

Not only do Foreign Objects not belong outside aircraft in their vicinity, they don't belong inside them either. Aircraft maintenance engineers go to enormous lengths to prevent tools, nuts, bolts and other components and loose articles from finding their way into places they don't belong. In the RAF, personal tool kits, beloved of maintenance engineers in every other field, are forbidden. Aircraft tools are either drawn from a tool store on signature, with the tool required to be signed back at the end of a shift before anybody is allowed to go home, or taken from a 'shadow-board' placed near an aircraft where every removed tool can be seen by its bright fluorescent 'shadow' that is revealed, showing what it is and where it is missing from. The personal tag of the tool's user is clipped in its place to show who has it. But in spite of all these and other precautions, the occasional Murphy still gets through. A passenger looking out of the window as a Boeing 737 landed at a British airport in 2002 was astonished to see a spanner resting in the reverse thrust mechanism of the starboard engine. He reported it to the ground staff who were even more surprised to find an adjustable wrench there too, keeping it company.

When you are a maintenance engineer working on an aircraft and you lose something, and you know it's there somewhere but you can't find it, what do you do? It's quite simple: you do find it, by whatever means it takes. You take out whatever equipment, furniture, fittings, components, etc. necessary until you reach it. If you are not sure where it is, you can try X-raying the aircraft to locate the object by taping photographic paper on the surface of the wing or fuselage, then firing X-rays through the structure by exposing a strong radioactive source in the appropriate direction. The radioactive material for this purpose is housed in a lead sphere, painted bright orange, with a mechanical window in the surface of the sphere that is operated remotely by a mechanical cable with a timer to give the correctly timed exposure of the source while everyone clutches themselves at a good distance away. About three hangars away feels about right. The whole arrangement is known as a Clockwork Orange, perfectly safe with its lead mechanical window closed, and aircraft engineers are always most happy to be asked to transport these devices in their cars. With the statutory 'Danger, Transporting Radioactive Material' signs on the front and rear of the car, the traffic just melts away. The skull and cross-bones picture helps. More than one RAF engineer, contemplating a long car journey to see his girlfriend, has begged to be allowed to keep the Clockwork Orange for the weekend. In vain I hasten to add - although it has occasionally been known for the car display signs to have become strangely mislaid until the Monday morning.

When, in spite of long and expensive efforts, a lost object in an aircraft just cannot be located and retrieved, the engineer responsible for the aircraft's airworthiness has a tough decision. After all, you cannot turn an aircraft upside-down in a hangar and shake it, tempting though that may be on many occasions. You cannot scrap a one hundred million dollar aircraft just because you think there is something in it that doesn't belong there - the accountants would hate you to the extent that they might even find another engineer with less expensive principles. So you have no real option but to sign off the aircraft as airworthy for a number of flights, then hunt again after that time when the offending object might have migrated somewhere where it can at last be discovered. In doing so, the engineer can console himself that, through careful design, modern aircraft are constructed in such a way that a foreign object should not be able to find its way into a position where it could jam a control run to a flying surface or an engine. After all, upwards of two hundred foreign objects walk on for every flight, most carrying another two or three foreign objects each. Murphy's Law still applies, however, and Sod's Corollary is ever-present. So the policy remains – known loose articles must be found and retrieved. There are just too many memories from the past of aircraft being lost and part of a control run being subsequently found in the wreckage, complete with the witness mark from the threads of the stray bolt at the point where it lodged in the controls and delivered its fatal jam...

If we can guard against loose article FOD by making sure our aircraft designs are careful and our engineering practices meticulous, what can we do about birds? To some extent we can design against birds. Bird-strikes on the airframe or the engines, while alarming and inconvenient, pose little danger to the aircraft as long as the birds are small. Strikes by large birds, however, are a significant hazard. A Vickers Viscount struck a 15lb swan at 10,000 feet over Maryland in the 1960s and all on board were lost. And as recently as December 1997 a British Airways Boeing 747 taking off from London Heathrow Airport collected a grey heron in the No. 2 engine, which caused the engine (and, definitely, the heron) to disintegrate. The crew coped with the emergency in exemplary fashion, however, and the aircraft landed safely back at Heathrow not even getting a mention on that evening's television news. The grey heron was positively identified as such by the Birdstrike Avoidance Unit at the government's Central Science Laboratory, people who are the unsung heroes of the aircraft birdstrike business because they can identify a bird species from the DNA of a scrap of feather. Know your enemy and you can build your defences.

All sorts of airborne schemes have been tried to persuade birds to get out of the way. Forward-facing flashing high-intensity lights were proposed some years ago, set to flash at the frequency that certain 'threat' species of bird would find uncomfortable and so try to avoid. The problems with such ideas are twofold. First, a different species of bird comes the other way and finds the light flashing at that frequency rather attractive, certainly not what was intended. Second, the reflected flash off nearby clouds can irritate the pilots to the extent of potentially being able to induce flicker vertigo, the building block of epilepsy. Definitely career-shortening for a pilot and therefore not a good idea.

The two areas of an aircraft most vulnerable to bird-strikes are the engines and the cockpit, and so the scientists and engineers at Farnborough and the National Gas Turbine Establishment at nearby Pyestock had great fun in the 1960s firing chickens at high speed from an air gun into engines and at different schemes of aircraft windscreen to find designs that were strong enough to resist bird-strikes. Before the more animal-loving and sensitive readers reach for their pens at this point to write to their MPs about the incontrovertible evidence in this book of past government-sponsored chicken torture in Hampshire, I hasten to add that the chickens were frozen ones bought in Sainsbury's. To achieve realism, they were allowed to thaw completely before being accelerated down the long tube of the gun (fowl-piece, surely?) for the flight of a lifetime. All in the name of aeronautical research and flight safety, both truly noble causes to which any chicken with a social conscience ought to be proud to aspire. The technique remains a standard test at the Rolls-Royce aero engine factory at Derby, although for engine development work they now use simulated birds made of gel and other non-putrefying material because it is both nicer and healthier to work with. For the actual certification tests, however, before a new design of engine can be granted its airworthiness certificate, the requirements stipulate that real bird bodies, weighing up to eight pounds each, are fired into the engine running at full power. Your airliner has to be Canada Goose-proof.

On airfields, all manner of means have been tried to induce birds to go elsewhere and the effort never stops. At Miami International Airport in 2003 there was a concerted effort to get rid of hares on the airfield. They posed no danger to aircraft, rather the other way round, but the hundreds of vultures that turned up to feed on 'runway-kill' hares were another matter. Five aircraft had struck vultures at Miami in recent years and the Federal Aviation Administration were very aware of the six deaths and 101 injuries that bird-strikes had caused in the USA over the past ten years. Removing birds' food is one option when meat-eaters are the threat, but as long ago as World War Two the RAF experimented with falcons to chase smaller birds away, and by 1965 the New Zealand Government was funding experiments with a radio-controlled model hawk at Auckland International Airport. By the 1960s the experiments in bird-scaring had also moved on to thunder flashes, flares (Very lights) and recorded distress calls of the bird species concerned in order to impart the message. These techniques have to be deployed and timed with great skill or the flock will rise up into the path of a passing aircraft and cause the very accident that the measures are trying to prevent. The taped distress calls worked well at first, but the birds soon got used to them. One very senior RAF officer visiting a unit was shown the new bird-squawking Land-Rover and engaged the crew in a conversation which he hoped was going to be a notch above his usual line of "how long have you been here?"

"These bird distress calls, Corporal", he said briskly, "do they work?"

"Not really, Sir." came the reply. "The birds on this airfield don't go 'tweet-tweet' any more, they just snort with derision."

With one particular aircraft in the 1960s the birds did a lot more than snort with derision rather than stay clear: if there was an engine running, they came in search of it. This tragic story illustrates just how many things have to be thought of when an aircraft is designed. The aircraft concerned was the Lockheed L-188 Electra, a medium-sized passenger airliner powered by four large turboprop engines. On 4 October 1960, an Electra took off from Boston Airport in the USA and flew for just seconds before total failure of all four engines brought it down. The examination of the wreckage showed that every engine had ingested a number of starlings and all four engines were so badly damaged they had failed catastrophically. At the time the occurrence was thought to be a fluke, but soon other Electra pilots noticed that starlings were gathering by the side of the holding point near the runway entry point and that it was clearly the aircraft that was attracting them. By 1962 two researchers at the FAA Aeromedical Research Institute in Oklahoma City, Mr John Swearingen and Dr Stanley Mohler, proposed a theory that birds were attracted to the Electra because the aircraft's Allison 501 engines made a noise like chirping crickets! Starlings are partial to crickets. They suggested that the aircraft's noise signature, even at idle power, was its Achilles heel. At exactly 13,820 rpm the compressor made a noise that a hungry starling would travel miles for. And, as the Allison 501 was a constant speed engine, the increased volume of the same noise at full power was sufficient to get a large number of starlings very excited indeed, enough to get airborne en masse and chase the promised feast. At first Swearingen and Mohler's theory was widely dismissed, but they were soon proved exactly right about the cause of the Boston accident. Once the installation of the Allison 501 in the Electra was modified, the problem went away. The aircraft continues to fly today, principally as a freighter and in its military guise as the Lockheed P3 Orion maritime reconnaissance aircraft in service with the US Navy and with many other navies and air forces all over the world. Aircraft noise can cause many emotions, but aircraft engineers have to remember that the wrong type of noise can cause bird-strikes, FOD and even the loss of the aircraft.

13

Howling from the Cowling

In the 1950s, when early jet aircraft such as the Comet and propeller-turbine aircraft such as the Viscount were introduced, it quickly became apparent that the aircraft industry had one problem that it had to do its utmost to solve: noise. That same sound of four jet engines that so entranced a four-year-old and his grandfather in Chapter 2 was similarly capable of entrancing grandfathers everywhere – but only on the first occasion the grandfather heard it. The second time it was "there's that noise again", the third time it was "isn't that a racket?" and thereafter it was fist-shaking time. To some extent the military's noise was excusable because people understood that the combat performance of the military's aircraft was all-important, but even then the RAF and USAF had to resort to propaganda in the shape of car stickers that proclaimed 'Jet Noise – the Sound of Your Freedom' to make the average man in the East Anglia street think twice before objecting automatically to the military's fast, low-level activities. Television newsreel footage of the occasional war like the Falklands or the Gulf helps explain that need, of course, but war is something of an extreme measure to take in order to persuade a few minds that aircraft noise in peace-time is necessary if a military pilot is to train realistically for the day he has to go into battle on our behalf.

With civil aviation there can be no such argument. Even someone who travels by air on business or just once or twice a year on holiday cannot be persuaded to accept that the convenience of air travel, when they need it, somehow should justify them having to put up with the noise it generates on the other three hundred-plus days of the year when everybody else needs to do it. During the Second World War the whole population got used to the sounds of piston-engines ("*theirs*, rasping and horrible; *ours*, deep and sweet - ah, the Rolls-Royce Merlin!") and so the propeller-driven airliners of the early post-war period didn't create much excitement. That is, beyond the more expensive addresses in the suburbs where the inhabitants considered it was their right to be shielded from all unpleasant aspects of daily life, piston engine rumbles included. The jets, however, with their high-pitched scream as they approached, sounded out in stark contrast to the friendly growl of the piston engines and were another matter. The more often and the more hours of the day and night that jet and turboprop airliners operated, the louder the protests became from the very large number of people who lived below their flight paths.

If you are a luckless aeronautical engineer in the noise suppression business and the managing director beats down your door one morning and demands that you make his current best-selling jet engine quieter, the easiest option frankly is to quit the business and start an organic farm shop or something. Noise, once it is endemic in a design, is very difficult to kill. Not impossible, but difficult. Great efforts went on in the 1960s developing 'hush kits' for existing engines. The word 'hush' was, by any admission, something of a triumph of marketing optimism over acoustic reality. While the noise monitors placed at the end of runways by the local civil authorities would celebrate the effect of such devices by producing nicely lower decibel noise figures for all to understand, the man in the street was far from convinced that they made one pennyworth of difference. Two Rolls-Royce Speys on a One-Eleven were so noisy they made your tummy rumble, hush kit or no hush kit. Not surprisingly the hush kits were designed so that the engine would register satisfactorily at the appropriate frequencies on the authorities' noise monitors, rather than to stop people's tummies rumbling. A step-change downwards in noise production was what was needed and that meant new engines with new noise suppression technologies, not fiddled-with old engines and arguable data.

But before you can solve a problem you have to understand it. Just what causes jet noise? Is it noise or is it noises, in the plural? Those questions were answered by much research work in the 1960s that ranged from the theoretical (by the universities and the National Physical Laboratory) to the practical (the National Gas Turbine Establishment at Pyestock in Hampshire, Rolls-Royce in Derby, NASA, General Electric and Pratt and Whitney in the USA, etc.). It turns out that jet engine noise has nearly as many sources as the jet engine has components, so its suppression is not a trivial matter.

Consider the noise you make when you blow on the sort of cheap whistle that comes out of a Christmas cracker. The wedge of the whistle splits the air you are blowing in two – a fast top layer, blowing out of the whistle, and a stationary lower layer, trapped in the whistle's body. The interface between these two streams travelling at different speeds produces eddies and these eddies are what make the noise. If you look into the front of a jet engine you see things that produce a very similar effect. There are rows (stages) of stationary blades (called stators) alternating with rows of rotating compressor blades and there are perhaps sixteen or more stages in all. Stators and compressor blades, if the compression is to be efficient, must pass very close to each other as the compressor rotates and unhappily this is exactly the ideal arrangement for the production of millions of tiny eddies and lots of intense, high-pitched noise. Whistles are, of course, designed to make a noise and the average child will become very successful at it all too soon. With the jet engine, compressor noise is an irritating by-product of the essential first part of the process - compression of the airflow. Over the years the engine design teams, like those of Rolls-Royce at Derby, have produced clever designs of compressor blade that both work efficiently and produce much less noise from the front of the engine.

Of all man-made devices, the jet engine must be one of the most anti-social. If it were a politician up for election, surely no one would vote for it. Not only does it scream unreasonably out of its front end, it makes a great deal of noise out of its back end too. At the back end, the jet efflux is going to give us the propulsive thrust we need to get the aircraft off the ground and drive it along, and we need to safeguard it. Alas, with a jet pipe discharging a tube of hot air at a very high speed, surrounded by a mass of air at a much lower speed, we have our cheap whistle situation back again – an intense layer of shear between two masses of air travelling at very different speeds. We can expect eddies all around the periphery of the jet, even bigger ones than those that came from the compressor and stator blades and hence producing a lower frequency sound, but with lots more energy because of the sheer size of the air mixing involved. Our scream from the front end has become a roar from the back. We must tackle the back-end noise with the same principle as that for the noise from the front end: we want to make the engine quieter, but we must achieve a noise reduction with minimum possible effect on the thrust it produces.

In the early days of noisy jets all sorts of solutions were tried. Round, sawn-off jet-pipes of the military fighter variety were shown to be particularly noisy because the jet hit the slower air in a very sudden way. Corrugated jet-pipes emerged on the early Boeing 707s where the mixing took place around a larger circumference and the gas flow at that point could be made slower. In British engines like the Rolls-Royce Avon fitted to the Comet airliner, small undulations, similar in principle to the vortex generators on the wings (Chapter 10), were riveted inside jet-pipes to make the jet turbulent and so mix with the air outside over a wider area and in a less sharp and noisy way. Some modern solutions for noise suppression are simple and clever. If you are lucky enough to be sitting near a window in a British Aerospace 146 or Avro RJ series aircraft, towards the back of the wing and in line with the exhaust of the engines, look carefully at the inner jet pipe of the nearest engine. It has a metal fillet of triangular cross-section welded all round its perimeter. This is a tiny vortex generator – it gets in the way of the airflow from the outer core of the engine and causes that flow to tumble and to become turbulent. When that turbulent flow mixes with the fast inner jet a moment later, the turbulence ensures that the noise that results is only a fraction of what it would have been if the inner jet had mixed with a smooth outer flow. The little welded metal fillet was a simple move by the engineers at Avco-Lycoming, the original designers of the engine, making their ALF502 engine one of the quietest in the world. As a result the BAe 146 airliner and its successors have been best sellers for BAE Systems and its partners, able to fly into noise-sensitive Californian regional airports nearly twenty years ago when no other jet aircraft could.

In Britain in the 1960s and 1970s, the Department of Trade and Industry sponsored much research activity to discover effective ways of suppressing noise. A particularly noisy engine was the Bristol-Siddeley Viper, the small jet engine fitted to the RAF's Jet Provost trainer. The joke in the RAF was that the throttle on the Jet Provost Mark 3 did not actually increase the thrust when you opened it, it just increased the noise from the back end and the aircraft carried on much as before. The JP3 throttle was therefore widely referred to as the 'constant thrust, variable noise lever'. A little unfair, perhaps, but it caused more than one young pilot to remember the engine's limitations and not to rely on it too much to produce a sudden forward arrow of thrust to fly him out of trouble. Pilots learning to become Qualified Flying Instructors at the RAF's Central Flying School, back on the Jet Provost Mark 3 after flying much hotter types operationally, found themselves opening the JP3 throttle in stunned disbelief. The RAF's neighbours in the villages around Little Rissington in Gloucestershire must have felt similarly stunned, but for a different reason. The Viper was therefore an ideal engine on which to experiment with noise suppression techniques and in 1978 Aero Flight at RAE Bedford pressed into use its wake-research aircraft, a twin Viper-engined Hawker Siddeley 125, for that purpose. A variety of shrouds, nozzles and other devices were designed and a special noise-monitoring station was placed on the top of the Severn Bridge. After ensuring that the aircraft remained safe and stable to fly and assessing the engine performance with each different bit of metalwork fitted, the RAE test pilots would then evaluate the noise-suppression success or otherwise of each scheme by flying the HS125 past the bridge along an accurate and controlled path so that the resulting noise could be recorded and analysed.

The Royal Aircraft Establishment noise programmes, led by Dr Tony Holbeach at Farnborough, also added much knowledge to the issue of airframe noise. Engines are noisy, yes, but if by some miracle they were to be made totally quiet, what noise would be left? The airframe itself travelling through the air must make a big rushing noise, but nobody knew how much, or what affected it for better or for worse. To find out, RAE used its VC-10 to evaluate the effect on noise of things sticking out from the airframe, holes in it, gaps between control surfaces, etc. Because stable conditions were needed to compare results from one run to another, the flights were all carried out in one day and each involved diving the VC-10, with all four engines idled, at a marked point on Thurleigh airfield at Bedford so that the noise monitoring equipment underneath the flight path could gather the data. Of course, at the point when the airfield and its target cross arrived in the aircraft's windscreen with a size and clarity that raised mild concern on the part of the test crew, the four Conway engines were opened up to maximum power and the aircraft climbed and turned into a smart circuit so that it could be put on the ground as quickly as possible for the next test case to be prepared: a hole taped up, a panel taken off, whatever. The flights continued all day. If there were any birds walking around the perimeter of RAE Bedford that day, expecting their usual relaxing time, they must surely have made rapid plans to go somewhere quieter, perhaps forever. The VC-10 at go-around power at low level is a noisy aeroplane. Some of the local residents, who were a great bunch of people who took a keen interest in RAE Bedford's research, probably felt the same way. By putting up with the racket that day, they too made a noble contribution to the knowledge gained on the sources of airframe noise.

Happily, the natural progression of jet engine design has made things easier rather than harder as far as noise is concerned, and that is not a common occurrence in technological progress. The development of the high bypass or big fan engine that is common today on all large jet aircraft has actually brought about benefits for noise at both ends of the engine. The core of these high by-pass fan engines is as potentially noisy as any jet engine of comparable size, but as a fan-driver it is smaller than it would have to be if it were doing all the work on its own. And the huge fan, positioned in front of the core compressor, helps block its noise by reducing the amount that escapes. Moreover, the large tube of medium speed air, travelling around the by-pass from the fan, acts as a shroud around the core jet at the back. This has two effects: the by-pass air reduces the noise the core jet makes (because the speed difference between the two airflows is less than that of a jet discharging next to outside air alone), and it helps mask it from a listener below. However, when the fan becomes really big, as it has on the largest Trent engines, noise from the fan itself becomes a problem. This noise has to be 'designed away' with some clever blade shapes in the same manner that the compressor was quietened and by special design of the lining of the fan shroud, described next.

By far the biggest leap forward in noise reduction for modern engines has been the development of the technology for these special linings, the 'acoustic liner'. Recent research using high speed computers to model three-dimensional airflows and complex shapes has enabled the ducts inside the engine around the compressors and turbines to be designed with resonant chambers and other noise-killing features, and to be lined with special materials and honeycomb structures that themselves absorb and dampen noise. A simple way to think of it is that the noise in the engine behaves like a hyperactive person: it bounces around inside the house for so long and to such an extent that eventually it hasn't the energy to go out. That explanation is hopefully amusing and memorable, but it belies the complexity of the mathematical modelling and engineering that have been necessary to achieve this result with a jet engine. The aero-engine design teams at Rolls-Royce and the other manufacturers have done amazing things. When you remember how shattering the noise was from an 11,000lb thrust Rolls-Royce Spey engine on a Trident or One-Eleven, consider now that an engine of similar power is 20 decibels, or 75%, quieter. A 10 decibel reduction halves the noise, so a 20 decibel reduction halves it and then halves it again. In terms of the acoustic or sound energy reaching the observer on the ground, 20 decibels represents a 99% reduction in energy. Quite remarkable. Current research promises to deliver another 10 decibel reduction within a few years. That will be a 99.9% reduction in sound energy compared with a 1970s engine of similar thrust. That is still not enough, though, and NASA in the USA has declared a goal for a further 20 decibel reduction below today's noise levels to be reached in twenty-five years time. Achieving that will almost certainly mean designing and building aircraft that will look very different from those we fly today and Chapter 19 gives a glimpse of that future. Work continues at Derby and elsewhere in the aircraft industry with relentless determination because aircraft noise is a major political issue, the biggest of all the environmental issues because voters feel affected by it most directly. If you look up 'aircraft noise suppression' on an internet search engine, you will not find details of the latest research into making aircraft quieter. Instead, you will find countless sites describing smaller, cheaper, more compact devices for monitoring the noise that aircraft make so that local authorities, even private householders, can set up their evidence-gathering activities. And you will find the trumpetings of people doing it. For them 'suppression' means 'monitor the noise and make the case for banning some flying', for they have no intellectual contribution to make towards solving the actual problem. They leave that to others. They are troubled souls, though, and simple humanity says that we should sympathise with those whose lives have become dominated by aircraft noise. That said, aircraft noise clearly affects some people more than others because, at London Heathrow Airport, thirty-three percent of the noise complaints come from just five people. Nearly half of the complaints, forty-five percent, come from the same twenty people. The Australians have a robust way of keeping sensitive people away from noisy areas. They log the addresses of people who complain about aircraft noise and they make the log available to people who are house-hunting. If aircraft noise is a particular issue with someone, they are of course entitled to know if it is a problem in the area where they might choose to live.

"Silence is Golden, Nigel!"

The aim of the aircraft design and aircraft engine fraternities must surely be to solve the noise problem, as they have solved others, so that comparative peace can be brought to airport neighbourhoods and noise is no longer an issue. Their ultimate aim should be for the need for aircraft noise monitoring equipment to disappear and for its makers to be forced to turn their manufacturing talents elsewhere. Quietly, of course.

14

Down Through the Murk

As air transport grew in the 1930s it dawned on the authorities that for it to be reliable as well as safe, there had to be a way of ensuring that aircraft could land in poor weather conditions. Tales of following railway lines in the fog and reading station names abounded, as well as ghostly stories like the one of the pilot who got lost and, low on fuel at night, desperately force-landed in a dark field. He climbed out, told his passengers to stay seated, and stumbled across the field toward the nearest light to ask where he was, only to be told 'Croydon Airport' - which was his intended destination! Definitely not the way to run an air transport system. The problems of operating in foggy Europe were further underlined by experiences in the Second World War when aircraft often arrived back over Britain at dawn to find the whole country fog-bound and with nowhere to land. One night, half of one Pathfinder squadron's bombers were destroyed when they were either abandoned by their crews in such circumstances, or crashed trying to land in the fog. If the flak and fighters didn't get you, there was always the good old British weather.

The early years after the War saw a determined effort to try to solve this problem. There had been major advances in electronics during the War, by both sides, and it was some of these technologies (such as the German Lorenz bomb-aiming beams) that were pressed into use. However, they could not deliver the accuracy needed near the ground and it was a wartime American development, the Instrument Landing System (ILS), that finally showed the required promise.

ILS radiates two flat beams, one horizontal and one vertical and therefore intersecting at right angles, up the required approach path for aircraft coming in to land. The effect is rather like someone grasping the sharp end of a dart and pointing the four tail feathers skywards. Equipment in the aircraft can detect when it is satisfactorily positioned on the cross-point of the beams, but the detailed design of the ILS signals also enables the aircraft to estimate how far away from that required intersection it is, and hence fly a path to 'capture' the centre. This was clearly a promising way ahead for automatic landings and in 1947 the UK's Blind Landing Experimental Unit (BLEU) was set up at Martlesham Heath in Suffolk to push things forward. This was a research initiative, funded by government in the days when the Common Good was perceived to be enough reason for moving technology forward and there was no need to enquire who else might be interested in paying. The airlines and the Air Ministry, with its forthcoming all-weather jet fighters and bombers, were to be the beneficiaries.

It was quickly apparent from BLEU's early work that, while the ILS had promise as a concept to assist blind landings, its beams were not stable or accurate enough to provide the sort of pinpoint guidance that an aircraft needed when close to the ground. In these days of micro-electronics it is sometimes difficult to remember that electronic equipment then consisted of very large racks of hand-soldered resistance, inductance and capacitance components connected by many wires to large thermionic valves. These valves had elements that had to glow red to produce electrons for the item to operate. Consequently, all the electronic racks used to become very hot. When electronic components (even wires) get hot their properties change and it is these changes that cause the instabilities, the jitters, which spoil the accuracy of the whole equipment.

From the beginning, the British effort recognised that safe landing in poor conditions meant a completely electronic automatic landing, rather than a system with a man in the loop (a pilot, under some stress) chasing some dot on an instrument. So it wasn't just the accuracies of the ILS beams that were of interest; it was how the autopilot fitted to the aircraft would react to the off-centre error signals that the beams produced and how the aircraft itself would respond to the signals that the autopilot gave it. The automatic landing system, therefore, was a system of many components, both ground-borne and airborne, all of which had to work together and talk to one another correctly if the whole thing was to work safely. For success, therefore, the various bits of the research establishments (the signals specialists, the autopilot developers and the flight dynamics people) also had to work together and talk to one another in a similar way.

The first 'fix' that was tried, to overcome the problems of jitter from the ILS beam, was a leader cable. This was in fact a pair of cables, fanning out from the runway threshold and continuing back for a length of well over a mile. Each emitted a magnetic field that a receiver in the aircraft could pick up, and the aircraft could be guided along the line that bisected the two cables, straight down towards the runway. The idea had been tried before to guide ships into harbour in foggy weather and the five mile long Ambrose Channel Piloting Cable was established in New York Harbour as early as 1920. The problem with leader cables around airports, however, was one of practicality. In the same manner that little things like quarries and Windsor Castle got in the way of very long runways, so inconveniences such as Hounslow got in the way of any idea of laying leader cables on the approaches to London Heathrow's western runways. The idea, although it worked, was a non-starter.

Instead, attention turned to ways of improving the ILS signal. The Radio Team at BLEU, comprising among others Keith Wood, Dick Vince and David Webb, developed a new ILS aerial that provided a much more stable and accurate beam. It was a large device and the first consisted of a large ring of poles with cable wound round them. The design was so successful that it was copied at major military and civil airfields all over Britain and one of the first was built at London Heathrow Airport.

The next problem to be solved concerned how to measure accurately the aircraft's height above the ground. Altimeters typically operate by sensing air pressure and converting that into a height measurement, either above sea level or above ground level. These barometric altimeters, however, are as accurate as the similar-sounding device in the hall: give them a tap and the needle jumps to overcome all the pent-up friction in the mechanism. Great for indicating tomorrow's weather, less great for establishing an aircraft's height above foggy ground to an accuracy of one foot. A radio altimeter was required, working like a downward-pointing short-range radar, but the best of these in the late 1940s was accurate only to about twenty feet. Here the BLEU Radio Team again triumphed when a group led by Alan Hammond developed a new radio altimeter that worked at microwave frequencies. This enabled height above the ground to be determined with the required accuracy and fed to the autopilot, which in turn could be programmed to execute a 'flare' as height decreased to zero so that the aircraft would arrive gently on the runway with just a small rate of descent. The device was a great success and all subsequent radio altimeters used in autoland systems to this day have been based on that design.

With the new radio altimeter fitted and with the new ILS aerial installed at Woodbridge airfield in Suffolk, next door to Martlesham Heath, the BLEU's twin-engined de Havilland Devon aircraft in the hands of test pilot Flight Lieutenant Noel Adams made the first fully automatic landing on 3 July 1950. This was the start of a painstaking blind landing development programme that had to take place before the technology could be deemed safe enough for the fare paying public.

But how safe was safe enough? One of the lovely things about engineering is that the discipline enables you to put firm numbers on the issue of risk, rather than just having the pointless and endless exchange of subjective views that usually passes for policy-making in a democracy. Numbers add tone to what would otherwise be a vulgar brawl. The Air Registration Board showed that, at that time, the world-wide accident rate to civil aircraft on scheduled services was one in one million. It was therefore decided that an acceptable performance for an autoland system would be that it should not be the cause of an accident in more than one in ten million landings, i.e. ten times better or more than the current experience. Unfortunately the press got hold of this figure and interpreted it as "being designed to kill people, once in ten million flights." Eventually public opinion was placated by a combination of a wise silence and the gently propagated notion that the design was actually intended specifically *not* to hurt anybody in at least 9,999,999 landings and that this was rather a lot, even if you flew for a living. The experience left the highly numerate BLEU researchers wondering how the members of some professions actually had the courage to get out of bed in the mornings. Or, looking at a different statistic, actually to go to bed in the first place.

But how to demonstrate the one in ten million? It was clear immediately that no one system could ever demonstrate that reliability and that some 'redundancy' was necessary so that a serviceable secondary system could take over if the primary one failed. Then the one in ten million could be derived from the whole system, the primary and its back-up. In the design and test work that followed, two philosophies emerged. The first was the 'triplex' system, used in the Smiths autopilot of Hawker Siddeley's Trident airliner. In this, three identical systems worked together and 'voted' constantly among themselves, discarding any one of the systems that disagreed with the other two. In the second philosophy, used by Elliott Automation (later GEC), the autopilot had two channels, each independently monitored. This scheme was used in the Vickers VC-10 airliner and later in Concorde. Over the years the companies' development work for each system proved to the Air Registration Board's satisfaction that both demonstrated the required reliability of a possible failure in less than one in ten million flights. In the past forty years, the flying experience of all those and other types of aircraft fitted with autoland systems has borne out this proof for real.

The very early test flying of the new autoland systems took place, of course, in perfect conditions. This was so that, if the system diverged from the ideal approach path, the test pilot could disconnect it and wrestle the aircraft away from the fate that his emerging technology apparently had in store for him that day. Gradually, of course, the design and engineering of the systems improved and confidence grew, and many thousands of automatic landings at Woodbridge, and later at BLEU's new home at Thurleigh near Bedford, were carried out in all sorts of ordinarily unflyable conditions. London Heathrow Airport was used on foggy days, when of course all normal flights were grounded and passengers sat in the terminals, fuming. One could imagine that their fumes turned to flames and smoke when they were treated, through the murk, to the sight and sound (or probably just the sound) of the ancient Vickers Varsity from BLEU carrying out perfectly safe landings on Heathrow's foggy runway with test pilots like Flight Lieutenant L. W. F. 'Pinky' Stark famously waving his hands above his head for the photographer sitting behind him. When passengers asked the ever-helpful airline service staff why they couldn't fly as well, doubtless they were totally satisfied with the answer, "I am sorry, but not until we demonstrate one in ten to the power seven, madam." Actually, these exercises revealed some unforeseen problems. On one occasion Flight Lieutenant Stark landed at Heathrow when it was so foggy he and the crew could not find the taxiway on which to taxi down to their dispersal for a well-earned cup of tea. They had to back-track down the runway centre line, turn round and take off again, and fly back to RAE Bedford for their tea. Clearly if autoland was to be a practical proposition for airline operations in zero visibility, some sort of ground taxi-guidance system would be needed as well.

By 1964 the development work was complete and all the safety goals had been demonstrated satisfactorily to the airworthiness authorities. Much work had been done over seventeen years to achieve these goals. ILS systems, thanks to BLEU's staff and some inspiring work by Standard Telecommunications and Cables (STC), were now projecting two razor blade-like beams into the sky. Autopilots were driving airliners down the prescribed narrow tube of the approach path, 'flaring' the aircraft to arrest its descent when the radio altimeters sensed the ground, and kicking off the drift due to cross-wind as the aircraft descended the last twelve feet to the runway surface. Auto-throttles controlled aircraft speed accurately throughout these manoeuvres, and ground roll-out guidance, developed by Geoff Harrison's team at BLEU, kept the aircraft straight and on the centre of the runway after it had landed. All the systems were those that BLEU had envisaged during its early work in the 1950s. The difference now was that they worked so well that the aircraft did not need a test pilot with his hands hovering a millimetre from the controls - it was happy with a line pilot wearing a short-sleeved white shirt and a huge smile. On 4 November 1964, Captain Eric Poole landed BEA Trident 1 G-ARPB at Heathrow in fog conditions that specified that his decision height was zero and the runway visual range was only fifty metres. By the early 1970s, when crews had been trained, qualified and gained more confidence using the system in clear conditions, BEA's Trident passengers were treated to routinely reliable on-time arrivals into a foggy London from whence all other airlines had diverted. During the nearly forty years that have followed, all the world's airliners have the automatic landing system and it is the one that Britain's BLEU developed. In day-to-day operations, autolands quickly became commonplace and originally were often carried out in good conditions so that the performance of the system could be monitored or calibrated, or so that pilots could develop their own confidence in the technique. Now, however, autoland systems are self-monitoring and self-calibrating and pilots have great confidence in them. When they need the autoland for real, as is often the case in Europe's winter weather, they can observe calmly their aircraft descending and landing with elegant predictability, with their chosen runway arriving under their aircraft's wheels through the fog, wind and rain (and pointing in the right direction) in true Relativistic style.

*"When it's foggy this is the **only** way to fly!"*

Even unequipped aircraft can benefit from autoland systems. At least, with the application of a little airmanship they can. Some years ago, one Sunday afternoon, a British Airways BAe 748 was airborne from Glasgow on an air test as part of the extensive requirement to renew the aircraft's Certificate of Airworthiness. After an hour, with the test schedule complete and darkness falling, the crew turned back towards Glasgow to be told that the weather had closed in and that they should consider diverting. The BA flight test crew didn't want to divert anywhere. It was a Sunday. They had only come into work on a Sunday because that was the best day for flight tests - you weren't allowed to fly anywhere in Scotland on a Sunday with fare-payers because it wurr a heathen thing tae do!   Where were they going to go? London? No thanks. Manchester? Heaven forbid. The aircraft had lots of fuel so the pilot elected to go into the Glasgow holding pattern and wait for his luck to improve. Glasgow air traffic control asked him for his intentions in vain. He just went round and round for an hour or so as it got colder and foggier and night began to fall. But he had a cunning plan.

Then, out of the south, came the half past five Trident schedule from Heathrow. It called up on Glasgow's approach frequency and was vectored for an ILS capture and autoland from the south-west. The 748 pilot then called for a positioning to land four minutes behind the Trident. Air traffic control advised him that the RVR (runway visual range) was below the 748's limits. The 748 pilot replied that, if that stayed the case when he was established on ILS on his final approach, he would go around and divert to Manchester. The Trident auto-landed ahead of him and, hey presto, the heat of the Trident's engines and its reverse thrust temporarily improved Glasgow's RVR to within the 748's limits by blowing the fog away! The smaller aircraft landed safely from a visual approach right behind it, and three minutes later Glasgow Airport went below RVR limits for a visual approach for the rest of the night. If you are an aviator, autoland can do you a power of good even if you don't have it. Especially on a Sunday afternoon, when all you want is to get home...

15

Science Makes for Safety

Shortly after the Second World War one country punched well above its weight in the contributions it made to aircraft safety. Very unjustifiably, it isn't the first that springs immediately to the arrogant Northern Hemisphere mind when technology is discussed. It is Australia. The world's air travellers owe an enormous debt to the foresight and initiative of Australian aeronautical scientists and engineers who were at the forefront of early post-war research into topics that turned out to be vital for aircraft safety. Australia, like the USA, has always been an air-minded nation, out of necessity when you consider the huge distances between populations in that country. For a graphic demonstration of that, fly from Sydney to Singapore in a Boeing 747-400, leaving Kingsford-Smith Airport in mid-afternoon and grab a window seat. It will be four hours of travelling at 500 mph, and nightfall, before you eventually cross the coast and see the lights at the north-western tip of Australia and head out over the sea. During that time you will have been able to count the signs of human habitation that you have seen out of the window just about on the fingers of your hands. Australia is big. It needs air transport, and from the 1930s onwards Australia's air services grew rapidly. By 1950 the Australian government had a thriving Aeronautical Research Laboratory (ARL) in Melbourne that was geared to the needs of future air transport in what promised to be a thriving post-war period.

One young ARL scientist, Dr David Warren, was a chemist who specialised in fuel tank explosions. He was closely involved with the ARL contribution to the early investigations into the losses of the Comet airliner when the cause was not known and fuel tank explosions seemed a strong possibility. The Comet was a puzzle. With evidence limited to transcripts of occasional radio messages and wreckage trawled up from the Mediterranean, and because there were no witnesses or survivors, Dr Warren realised that much more might have been known had there been some way of recording the conversations in the cockpit, more still had there been a recording of the aircraft's systems and instruments during the minutes leading up to the accident. David Warren was sensitive to the need for such things. When he was just nine years old his father had been killed in one of Australia's earliest air disasters, the loss of the DH86 Express VH-URN *Miss Hobart* in the Bass Strait off Victoria on 19 October 1934. So in 1954 David wrote a scientific paper about the usefulness of an airborne recording device and, in the best traditions of aeronautical scientific progress, no notice was taken of it at all. Undaunted, and remembering the power of 'show and tell' from his schooldays, he built the world's first accident data recorder in his own time and presented it to his ARL masters in 1957. It would store up to four hours of cockpit conversations, plus readings from the flight instruments. But no one loves a prophet in his own country and the Australian aviation authorities were at best lukewarm to the idea. He was, however, asked to show his recorder informally during a visit to ARL by Air Vice-Marshal Sir Robert Hardingham, the Secretary of the Air Registration Board, the authority for air safety in the UK. Sir Robert was immediately enthusiastic and young Dr Warren was on a plane to England the following week with his 'Flight Memory'.

The British love a good idea, doubly so when it comes from abroad, and Dr Warren's box was no exception. During his visit he and his box made an appearance on television, and even on the BBC's prime-time *Radio Newsreel*. The British authorities indicated their intention to make such devices mandatory in large public transport aircraft and many UK manufacturers offered their support. In the UK, Bill Penny at the Aeroplane & Armament Experimental Establishment at Boscombe Down in Wiltshire and James Giles at the de Havilland Aircraft Company must have wondered why the powers-that-be were suddenly very interested in the work they had been doing together on airborne data recording since 1955! The Penny and Giles scheme, which was intended primarily to assist flight testing, recorded even more sophisticated data than did Dr Warren's box, such as control positions and accelerations. Like most good ideas, this one of airborne data recording was in fact sprouting all over the place. Back at ARL in Melbourne, Dr Warren was given a small team comprising Lane Sear, Ken Fraser and Walter Boswell, and together they improved their unit to record the aircraft's instruments more accurately and at twenty-four samples per second. The British firm S. Davall and Son approached ARL for the production rights and their famous 'Red Egg' crash recorder using fire-resistant wire as the recording medium was the result, winning a major part of the world market as demand grew. Not in Australia, however. It took the unexplained crash of Trans Australia Airlines Fokker Friendship VH-TFB in Queensland on 10 June 1960, and the recommendations of the judge heading the inquiry, before the Australian authorities finally mandated recorders in their aircraft. Ironically, because of a judicial order, Australia then became the first country actually to make cockpit voice recorders compulsory, but it was 1967 before that actually happened because the first solution they had chosen (magnetic tape) was not sufficiently fireproof.

In Britain, the Davall 'Red Egg' was fitted to a few aircraft for evaluation purposes. From the very start, aircraft flight data recorders have been painted bright red so that they can be found easily after an accident, although we can be confident that in a thousand years from now people will still refer to them as the 'black box'. This is a comforting euphemism for people who do not know what goes on inside such a device, who know that they never will, but who somehow find it reassuring that something of that nature should be looking after their collective welfare. 'Black boxes' are mysterious. A professor of aeronautical engineering at one of Britain's universities kept one on his desk and ascribed magic powers to it. No student was allowed to touch it, especially to touch the switch on its side. It was the professor's precious 'black box' and it was to be left alone. Inevitably it became a constant distraction during tutorials and the subject of much speculation among the professor's students. At long last the professor went on leave for a week. On some pretext, some third year students got hold of his door key from his secretary and stole into his office, bent on scientific investigation. After a short discussion they plucked up the necessary courage and operated the small switch on the side of the magic 'black box'... There was a whirring noise and a small green hand came out of a flap on the side of the black box, turned off the switch and went back in again!

The first two Red Eggs were fitted to Vanguard airliners of BEA and, entirely by coincidence one night in October 1965, both were trying to land at London Heathrow in the fog. On its third attempt to land, Vanguard 'Echo Echo' (G-APEE) crashed on to the runway, well along its length, in a pronounced nose-down attitude. There was no evidence that anything had fallen off in flight and, if there had been no flight recorder, the conclusion from such an impact and aircraft attitude would most likely have been that the aircraft had stalled and had hit the ground as the nose pitched down following the stall. However, the Red Egg flight recorder told a very different story. Although in those days only a few flight parameters were recorded on the wire and the sampling rate wouldn't catch things that occurred many times a second, the data was clear that the aircraft had climbed several hundred feet yet the pilot had progressively pushed the control column forward until impact. One of the causes identified was an aeromedical one in that both pilots had disbelieved their instruments and had believed their senses. Unfortunately their senses had been wrong. Detailed analysis of the recorded wire, which had shattered and had to be painstakingly re-assembled at Farnborough, showed that the aircraft's acceleration as it climbed away would have given the captain and his co-pilot the erroneous impression that they were pitching upwards towards the vertical. They would have become thoroughly disoriented through no fault of their own. Whole new lessons were learned from that accident: about interpretation of instruments, about the limitations of simulators that cannot accelerate, and about the weaknesses of the human inner ear in interpreting acceleration. All these things could be (and were, subsequently) countered by specific training.

Thousands of people now pay money to get fooled by these and similar effects on rides at Disney and other theme parks: riding up a ramp in the dark in a small chair, with faster and faster moving scenery being projected around you, you become convinced that you are accelerating to a hundred miles per hour or more - before you emerge through a hole in the screen to discover that the chair is only doing 2 mph! Fun at Disney, but such spoof effects on the poor inner ear and brain are deadly serious in an aeroplane on a foggy night. The flight data recorder first proved its worth on Vanguard 'Echo Echo' because it provided both the answer to an obscure accident and the lessons to prevent other accidents of a similar kind. Since then flight data recorders, and subsequently cockpit voice recorders (eventually in Britain, after recommendations following another accident in 1972), have become mandatory on every large passenger aircraft. They provide the first strand of evidence (but *only* the first strand, see the next chapter) to an investigation after an accident. Indeed, if television newsreaders reporting a new accident do not mention that investigators are looking for the 'black boxes', people have been known to ring up the station and insist that the news staff pass on their helpful suggestion to do so.

In Britain the recorders soon started to provide rather more than accident data. The new, highly swept-wing jet airliners of the early 1960s were very different from their propeller-driven predecessors, even from the modestly swept-wing Comet, and they brought new worries and new problems for airline operations. The Air Registration Board (forerunner of the CAA) and scientists at the Royal Aircraft Establishments at Bedford and Farnborough realised that the recorded data could tell them how aircraft were actually operated day-to-day, what sort of flight conditions they experienced and when they might be at risk. To improve scientific knowledge of an aircraft's environment, a special flight data recorder was fitted to some airliner types in what became known as the Civil Aircraft Airworthiness Data Recording Programme, or CAADRP. RAE Bedford examined the operational issues of airline flying and Farnborough looked at the implications for the aircraft's structure. Soon it became clear that the items of most interest were the unusual or unexpected things, when a parameter (for example the rate of descent of the airliner) went beyond the permitted range that had been set for it. The system was set up to record the flight data either side of these 'events' and print them out for the analysts. The 'what?' was on the printout trace, together with the flight data before and after it, but then the 'why?' had to be investigated. Other data then had to be gathered about the occurrence, such as weather details and other factors that might have been present. Some might have been recorded in a crew logbook. Where questions still remained, the crews concerned were also brought into the discussion and much was learned. The overall picture that has emerged from CAADRP is that of the true reality of jet airliner operations. Much credit is due to the CAA and the RAE for the programme and to the scientific teams at Farnborough and Bedford for their painstaking study and analysis of many thousands of feet of computer paper output produced by the airlines' recorded data. But great credit is also due to the pilots' union, the British Air Line Pilots Association (BALPA), who are one of the most technically aware organisations of their kind in the world and who gave the programme their full backing. CAADRP has made a major contribution to the design for safety and operation of all subsequent aircraft types, including of course the Concorde. The lessons learned from the programme have even shaped practices in air traffic control: controllers know the characteristics of the aircraft types they are controlling and do not instruct pilots to fly any profile outside what they know to be the comfortable operating parameters of the type concerned.

In the aftermath of the Second World War the Australians, like all the Allies, had very many combat aircraft that were surplus to requirements. One of their scientists, Alfred Payne, saw a vital use for all those old aircraft before they went to museums or to the scrap merchants. He realised that with these unwanted aircraft he had the means to explore some of the factors that caused a particularly dangerous phenomenon that had asserted itself during the War: metal fatigue. Fatigue cracks can cause a wing or other structure to fail in flight under a perfectly normal and unexceptional load and at an unpredictable time. During the War such things had happened in surprising and unexplained ways. If post-war air transport was to be safe, scientists and engineers had to be able to understand all the factors that led to the onset of fatigue failures in steels, alloys and other materials that were used for constructing aeroplanes, and thus be able to design against them.

In particular, the investigation that followed the unexplained loss of the Comet 1 airliner G-ALYP on 10 January 1954 when the aircraft disintegrated at altitude and fell into the Mediterranean Sea near Elba, showed the need to know accurately both the loads being experienced by an aircraft and the effects those loads would have. Parts of new aircraft were tested in static test frames that confirmed they could reach their 'design' load, i.e. the extreme load that was designed to break them. But to test a type's resistance to a lifetime of fatigue loads, i.e. the everyday alternating loads that resulted from pressurising the cabin, from gusts, control surface movements, etc., and which occurred throughout the aircraft's service, a whole aircraft (brand new, from the production line) had to be tested in a huge dynamic fatigue test rig. The Comet experience had shown that for a jet airliner that spent most of its time flying high in smooth air, the pressurised cabin was a very vulnerable part. RAE Farnborough developed a standard fatigue test for airliner cabins by repeatedly pressurising them with water when they were mounted in a tank. Water was chosen because, when it releases its pressure as a failure occurs, it causes little further damage. The Concorde's fatigue test rig at Farnborough, however, had to be more complicated and use air because, as well as other flight loads, the test airframe had to suffer the stresses from the structural heating that resulted from supersonic flight. But by the time the 1960s airliners and the Concorde came along, engineers knew how to derive with confidence from the fatigue test results a safe 'life' between inspections for an aircraft and how and where to look for any cracks. This life (or 'lives', if individual components were concerned) would be expressed in numbers of flights, in flying hours, or even in the number of take-offs and landings. Prediction of fatigue life from fatigue tests was the area in which Alfred Payne and other researchers made such important contributions in the early post-war years.

Alfred Payne and his team built a test frame in which a total of 222 wings from the surplus RAAF Mustang fighters were subjected to repeated varying loads, and these were applied in addition to the simultaneous constant load that represented level flight. Eventually all the wings failed from fatigue, a fact that could be confirmed by examining the failed fracture surfaces through a microscope. Fatigue cracks are quite distinctive – in aluminium alloy they appear as hundreds of striations or 'tide marks' that occur as the fatigue crack spreads slowly across the fracture surface. Once the fatigue crack grows to the extent that the un-cracked part of the metal is no longer strong enough to bear the constant load, the component fails with a bang. What interested Alfred was the fact that all the fatigue life results were different. Identical wings, identical loads, but the results showed clearly different fatigue lives with different numbers of cycles-to-failure. It turned out that small variations in manufacturing detail, in metal qualities and in many other factors were causing the results to vary greatly, to give them a 'scatter' – he had a few early failures and a few wings that lasted for an unusually long time, but more wings failed around some clearly definable mean value of life. He and other aircraft scientists working on the problem reasoned that the estimates of fatigue life obtained by a single test of a new type of aircraft in a test frame could not safely be regarded as representative of the life that all the production aircraft would enjoy in airline service. To be safe, you had to assume that the single aircraft test specimen had actually given you one of the *better* lives that would have been obtainable from a number of test specimens. You needed a safety factor.

As Alfred and his Australian colleagues tested to destruction all their 222 Mustang wings during the 1950s and published their results, other teams in the aircraft industry and at RAE Farnborough were also working to determine the proper safety factors. Roland Heywood and his colleagues at Farnborough collected data on the fatigue performance of large numbers of specimens representing the fatigue-critical features of aircraft structures and W.A.P. "Wapp" Fisher analysed their data statistically. Harold Parish, working for Hunting Aircraft Ltd in Britain, tested a number of wings and components from ex-RAF Piston Provost trainers. He had an advantage over Alfred Payne in that the RAF had monitored the loads on the Piston Provost wings during their flying service using RAE's acceleration-counting fatigue meters, so Harold knew their individual load-histories before he started testing. Consequently the scatter he discovered in his test results was much narrower than that from Payne's work. Alfred Payne's wings were of unknown provenance and some of them, it was discovered later, had been worked hard and significantly fatigue-damaged in service. But the data from both experimenters added to the fund of knowledge being obtained from mathematical analysis and other work, and eventually two safety factors began to emerge that satisfied the airworthiness authorities.

They were something of an eye-opener. Where a piece of structure could be monitored in some way, so that you had an accurate idea of *exactly* what load history it had actually experienced, the work showed that the safety factor you had to apply to the demonstrated life was three and one third. But where the component had just an estimated load history, where the load couldn't be directly monitored, that safety factor went up to five. This meant that a test specimen of a new airliner that broke in the fatigue test frame after having had repeated cycles of loads that simulated, say, 15,000 flights, actually indicated that the real airliner with passengers was only safe for a service life of 3,000 flights. This explained why training aircraft and bombers during the War had occasionally suffered structural failure in flight, well in advance of the life that the type's fatigue test had predicted. It explained why the Comet 1 had been unsafe and why the state-of-the-art fatigue testing applied to it at the time had not predicted its fatal weakness in service. And it explained how fatigue performance had, has, and always will have, absolutely nothing to do with the ordinary static strength of an item which is much more repeatable and predictable.

In the 1960s, this and other work from various nations was combined into a firm set of principles on which all future aircraft fatigue tests could be conducted. In the years since, new mathematical techniques of fracture mechanics have emerged, together

110

with new methods of detecting smaller and smaller cracks in airframes and engines, and the methods of assuring the structural health of aircraft have become ever more precise. The new knowledge has proved that the early results of the Australian and British researchers into aircraft fatigue did indeed provide a sound basis for safe operations. Millions of air passengers all over the world have enjoyed, and continue to enjoy, safe flying as a result of their work.

Knowing exactly how your aircraft are operated is important for safety. Both the military and the airlines now measure what happens to aircraft in day-to-day service. Many years ago, RAF Buccaneer jet strike aircraft began to suffer unexplained cracks in their fins. This came as a total surprise because the fatigue test on the aircraft had predicted nothing of the kind. It had correctly included the application of all the horizontal gust loads that an aircraft of that type should experience at low level and the safety factor that went with it. In vain the manufacturers examined the fin of the fatigue specimen, which was still at the factory. There was no sign of cracking or other fatigue damage. Being one of the RAF's more venerable aircraft, the Buccaneer had no operational data recording so the RAF specialist engineers responsible for it went to visit the squadrons to try to find out why the fins were suffering. The answer came, like so many, over a coffee in a crew-room.

"No we never touch the rudder," said one pilot. "We don't have to on jet aircraft except occasionally in a crosswind landing and that's not often." "Oh," he added with a sudden thought, "but we do when it rains."

"When it rains?" Squadron Leader Clive Ellam put down his coffee and it was just as well he did because he would have dropped it a few seconds later.

"Yes. When you are charging along, low level at five hundred knots in the rain, the damn windscreen wiper only cleans half the windscreen. So you have to give the aircraft a big bootful of rudder to get the airflow behind the wiper blade and, voila!, a clean windscreen!"

That was the answer. For lack of a powerful enough windscreen wiper motor, RAF Buccaneer pilots were applying repeated and huge loads to the aircraft's fin by ruddering their way across the countryside at high speed in the rain. The manufacturers at Brough on Humberside calculated the loads this would cause, then the fatigue life that would result from those loads applied so many times per minute to the fin on thirty percent of flights (the rainy ones). Another 'voila!' The calculated fatigue life tallied. The resulting modification programme to restore the Buccaneer fin's integrity was a great deal more expensive than a stronger wiper motor would have been at the start of the aircraft's service life. As it was, of course, the Buccaneer needed the new wiper motor in addition to the reinforced fin structure, to prevent the same thing happening again. Now, all major RAF aircraft types have at least a few operational squadron aircraft instrumented to discover exactly 'what's going on'. It is a sound investment. But you do need a few aircraft fitted, rather than just one or two. Early in the Tornado's production run, the Treasury over-ruled the RAF engineers' strong request that two aircraft in each of the Tornado's roles should be instrumented. This was important because the gauges and other sensors needed for monitoring can only be fitted inexpensively as the aircraft is built. "One in each role is enough", they said, after a long argument. In the maritime strike role, guess which was the first Tornado to be lost in an accident after just a few weeks' flying? Yes, it was the sole instrumented one. Treasury officials undoubtedly have impressive degrees from some of our better universities, but that education seems not to cover Sod's Corollary to Murphy's Law. Sadly, it seems also not to cover the principle that it is wise to accept honest, professional advice when dealing with an area outside one's own particular expertise.

16

Accidents Tell the Whole Truth

A Flight Safety poster in the RAF reads: 'Lonely? Bored? Want to meet all sorts of very intense and stimulating people? Try having an ACCIDENT!' Typical military sarcasm, you are probably thinking, and at best I suppose it is heavy irony. But it's true. All sorts of people suddenly take great interest in you, your abilities (especially your lack of them) and your performance, as well as those of your aircraft, when you have an accident. It's the findings and recommendations from accident inquiries that bring forth the policies, the money and the motivation for the changes that are needed to make things safer. Many would say it is those alone. Vision, genius, professional opinion (however well expressed), all these seem to count for little when expenditure of money might be the consequence. If you want things to change, say the cynics, wait for someone to have an accident.

While the next chapter of this book shows that many people are trying to ensure that this is no longer the case, it is true and very sad that almost all the thousands of systems, features and operating procedures to be found on a modern aircraft today are there because, at some point, someone somewhere came to grief for the lack of them. Automatic landing systems are now commonly fitted because aircraft like Vanguard 'Echo Echo' (Chapter 15) crashed while trying to land in poor visibility. Ground Proximity Warning Systems (GPWS) exist because someone collected a tree rather spectacularly in a Boeing 747's undercarriage on the approach to Nairobi, and left a few tyre marks in the bush as well, before going on to make a safe landing at the airport a few miles further on. It was even said for a while, in one airline that had something of a conscience about that incident, that GPWS stood for 'Game Park Warning System'. Disc brakes, anti-skid systems, reverse thrust, static structural tests, fatigue tests, just to highlight the things this book has been able to cover (and there are many more) – all came about because of accidents and incidents and people's resolve to prevent them happening again. It follows that, in the early years of aviation, many aircrew and their passengers were injured and killed in the process of making flying safer for those who followed. The aircrew and passengers who fly today without such risks owe them a debt. And the professional who operates aircraft today and who sees a new danger, surely owes it to those people's memory and to the aviation profession to do everything possible there and then about that new danger, before an accident happens.

Happily, people have often survived accidents to tell what went wrong. But often with aviation accidents there has been no one left to tell the tale and all that remains are eyewitness reports, the aircraft recorders and much wreckage. The finding-out of the true cause(s) of an accident and the shaping of the recommendations to prevent a recurrence are the responsibilities of the accident investigators, a small group of experienced former operating pilots and engineers in each country who bear a large part of the responsibility for keeping the aviation community's flying safe and ensuring it becomes ever safer.

The science, many would say the art, of accident investigation grew up during World War Two, when the sheer volume of air operations ensured a matching number of accidents. As accidents happened for which causes were obscure, so the investigators invented and discovered techniques that led them to the causes and so solved the mysteries. Today, the investigation professionals at the Air Accidents Investigation Branch (AAIB) at Farnborough in the UK, at the National Transportation Safety Board (NTSB) in the USA and at other bureaux across the world, have hundreds of techniques to use in their search for the causes of every accident.

The public, of course, are wedded to the usefulness of the 'black boxes'. But where a flight data recorder (FDR) and a Cockpit Voice Recorder (CVR) can sometimes give you all the information you need, often they will not. The FDR only samples a set number of parameters, and those at only a certain number of times per second. Suppose something like a hydraulic jack that operated a wing flap failed, and as a result the flap started to flutter in the airflow at many hundreds of times per second before it subsequently broke away half a second later. The FDR might sample the flap's position once during that time, or not at all. Whatever position it was occupying at the instant it was sampled, that position information about it from the FDR is unlikely to be of much help to an investigation. The CVR might be of more use because it might record the sound of the first break, the buzz and the second break as first the jack and then the flap itself failed, but remember the recorder and the failure are in different parts of the aircraft and the CVR is designed to pick up sounds on the flight deck, nothing more. So data recorders are useful, sometimes vital, but they often can only be used as corroborating evidence for some other indication of what went wrong. That other indication is often in the wreckage, but it might be an eyewitness's evidence or a video of a radar picture. A disciplined imagination and an ever-open and questioning mind are the qualities of a successful investigator.

A comprehensive description of investigation techniques, however interesting, is inappropriate here, but there are some examples from investigations that have lessons both for the general public and for members of the emergency services who might one day find themselves close to an accident site. When an air accident investigator arrives at a crash scene, his or her first question is, "Have I got the whole aircraft here?" That question is often not easy to answer in a sea of mud and fire engines, but the news that other items have been found a few fields or miles away will indicate that something came off the aircraft in flight. Those pieces are likely to be of more initial interest than the tons buried in soft mud at the main wreckage site. When Concorde F-BTSC crashed near Paris on 20 July 2000, the marks and bits left on the runway at Aéroport Charles de Gaulle were at least as important to the initial investigation as the smoking wreck at the disaster scene near the hotel at Gonesse, a few miles to the west.

A similar situation faced investigators when they arrived at the scene of a total accident to BEA Vanguard G-APEC near the village of Aarsele in Belgium on 2 October 1971. Pieces of the aircraft, large and small, were found both nearby and miles away. In those circumstances an investigator will log, on a large-scale map, exactly where each piece is found. He will then examine the marks it made as it struck the ground to discover which way up it was falling as it descended through the air. This is why it is so important for wreckage to be left exactly where it falls, and *as* it fell – fire-fighters and police, please note. (It is every accident investigator's nightmare to arrive at an accident site to find the wreckage assembled into a neat pile with a couple of people standing guard, holding brooms and wearing proud smiles.) The investigator will weigh each piece of wreckage and estimate the cross-sectional area that it presented to the airflow as it came down. He can then estimate the speed at which it fell. As it fell, the wind at the various altitudes it passed through will have blown it sideways, and putting these two speeds together will enable the investigator to plot its path backwards through the air, upwards and up-wind as it came down. The trajectories of scattered pieces will intersect where major assemblies disintegrated in the air and the earliest failure in that sequence will point the investigator towards the cause of the accident.

In the BEA Vanguard's case, the earliest pieces to have failed proved to have been the skin of the tail-plane at the back of the aircraft. With no tail surface capable of providing the down-force needed for stable flight, the aircraft had dived into the ground from a great height with the loss of all on board. From their fracture marks and their peeled shape, all the tail-plane skins seemed to have failed outwards like a bursting balloon, an unheard-of failure. What could have caused that? More investigations showed that the inside of the tail-plane could have become pressurised with air that had leaked from the cabin. Excavations from the main accident site revealed that the rear pressure bulkhead from the cabin had a small, corroded hole in its rim. The hole had allowed the pressurised cabin air to leak into the tail-plane's structure and to blow it up like a balloon, until it burst. The cause of the corrosion was found to be an acidic mixture that had formed from condensation and, amongst other things, tobacco smoke.

Today, when smoking is banned in aircraft cabins on the more safety-aware airlines, some of the passengers complain of having their 'rights' violated. It would seem, however, that the sixty-three people who perished in Belgium that day, due at least in part to all the smokers that had gone before them in the aircraft, had their rights violated rather more. Corrosion induced by tobacco and other acids in aircraft will always be a problem, although design standards have changed since the Vanguard accident and tail-planes and other un-pressurised structures attached to pressure cabins now have vent holes designed into them. Murphy's Law again: if it can happen it will, sometime, so design against it when it does. It is a shame that these lessons have had to be learned in such a hard way, but for every disaster that does occur, dozens more are prevented by inspired lateral thinking at the design stage or during operations by very aware operators. But there is a limit on the human race's ability to think perversely, even on engineers' ability to think that way (although some would dispute that).

Sometimes an accident happens to an aircraft that is so severe that it suffers forces and loads so large that none of the standard sensors that feed its flight data recorder (or 'black box') can measure them. Investigators have the wreckage, but they also look for anything else they can find to tell them the answers to their questions. Such an accident happened to BOAC Boeing 707 G-APFE near Mount Fuji in Japan on 5 March 1966. The aircraft had just left Tokyo for Hong Kong and was climbing to its cruise altitude. It was apparent from the wreckage of the wings that the aircraft had suffered some sort of gross over-load, but exactly how much was beyond the capability of any of the aircraft's systems to measure. However, the investigators found the answer in, of all places, a passenger's movie camera. The pilot had deliberately flown the aircraft near Mount Fuji to give the passengers a better view. One passenger was filming the mountain from a starboard window and his camera and film were recovered intact from the crash site. The film, when developed, showed that the camera had moved progressively downwards as the aircraft suffered a sudden acute vertical acceleration, or 'g'. Then the camera had jammed pointing at the floor with the button still pressed. Back at the AAIB at Farnborough a number of these cameras were acquired, loaded with film, taken to the Institute of Aviation Medicine and put in a centrifuge, the huge whirling arm that is used for research into aircrew's tolerance of high levels of 'g'. All the cameras jammed at exactly the same load, which gave some confidence to the assumption that the aircraft had suffered the same. What was amazing was that the load was ten 'g', or ten times the force of gravity. As the Boeing 707 wing was good for three and a half 'g' and stressed to fail at a value of five to six, it was hardly surprising that the wing had failed when it did. The pilot, in trying to give his passengers a special view, had flown into the lee of the mountain when a strong wind was blowing across its slopes. From a passenger's movie camera (that also showed the exact point over the ground where the mid-air break-up happened) and from a new technique developed by the accident investigators, it was proved that the aircraft had encountered gust turbulence way beyond its design limits and that this had caused the Boeing to disintegrate with the loss of all on board. The accident also sparked research into the turbulence that occurs behind conical shapes such as volcanoes in strong winds and it proved that such places are no-go areas for aircraft. Sure enough, the point where the Boeing came to grief was the very spot where the maximum turbulence from the mountain would have been encountered. The pilot of the Boeing 707 had no way of knowing this as he did his best for his passengers that crisp March morning. Nowadays, no pilot would be permitted by air traffic control to stray from the designated airway into what is now known to be a very dangerous area.

Just imagine, however, if some thoughtless person had found that movie camera either in the wreckage or nearby and, finding it working and clearly of no use to its owner, had 'liberated' it. Its vital evidence would have been missed. Perhaps it would have taken the crash of another airliner in the lee of a mountain for the root cause of the earlier Boeing 707's loss eventually to be discovered. Accident investigators are an imaginative and inventive bunch, as they showed here, but they cannot deploy their genius in unusual circumstances if people thoughtlessly walk off with the evidence or otherwise interfere with it. And the only people able to judge what is and what isn't evidence in any accident are the investigators.

Accident investigations produce the whole truth, some parts of which are often uncomfortable. When accident reports are published, all the failings of the people, processes and equipment involved are laid bare for professional and public scrutiny. In one hundred years of manned flight, accidents have taught us lessons that have undoubtedly led to better systems, sounder practices, higher standards, more effective training and education, improved airmanship in the shape of keener awareness of paths that have led to disaster, and a host of other benefits. However, these benefits have occurred largely because the culture of aviation has been an open one of learning, communication and progress. Aviation people have no natural leaning towards the type of culture that is negative and defensive, a way of life of cover-ups, blame and compensation. If safety is to keep improving, aviation's positive culture must continue and even be reinforced, and not diverted by a fashionable public hunger for blame. In particular, aviation must resist the influence of saddened but vindictive people who are possessed only of the smaller picture, the one ultimately depicting large amounts of money falling into their pockets which they imagine will make them feel better about their loss. Those who would seek compensation from disasters will not easily be persuaded that their actions might, in themselves, be compromising safety. But they, should reflect that, while the facts behind major accidents are well researched with public money and freely available to them, more minor incidents that did not lead to a disaster will only ever be publicised, and therefore acted upon, if they can be communicated in a way that is free from threat of recrimination. Because it is incidents, when they are properly reported, handled, followed up and publicised, that prevent accidents happening in the first place. 'If you wish for success, celebrate your failures' is a modern management principle. Aviation has been doing that for over one hundred years and, for everybody's sake, it needs to be allowed to continue to do so.

17

Listen and Learn

Any accident, whether on the ground, at sea or in the air, is an accident too many. Aircraft accidents, however, are particularly shocking and newsworthy, and consequently aviation has developed as strong a culture, or way of life, in safety and accident prevention as can be found in almost any other human activity. Over the years, very many air accidents that might easily have happened have been prevented by actions that aviation people took months or even years before. In some ways an aircraft is just like any other vehicle in that the margin can be tiny between what would have been an accident and what was actually a close shave. When you have a near miss in a car, almost always when you or someone else has had a lapse of judgement, you give a long low whistle and drive on for a few hours (or days or minutes, depending on the severity of the scare) being a bit more careful. With an aircraft, however, the 'near misses' in question are not necessarily close encounters of the colliding kind. In aircraft terms a 'near miss' might be the discovery of a large crack in some vital component during an inspection where, had the aircraft flown subsequently without it being discovered and fixed, a disaster would have happened very soon afterwards. So when something happens to your aircraft you have an obligation that you don't have after an incident in your car: you must quickly tell everybody who might also be affected by a similar problem. Everybody else with your type of aircraft or engine needs to know what has gone wrong, together with as much information as possible about how and why. You must do all you can to prevent them coming to grief through discovery of the same problem in a much harder way. If you fail, think how you will feel. If someone in the aviation business failed you, by sitting on some knowledge that cost you an aircraft and the people in it, what respect would you have for them?

All well-run aviation organisations have reporting systems so that incidents can be investigated, remedial measures taken, and the whole story publicised within the aviation safety community for everybody's benefit. The RAF's flight safety magazines inform everybody in the Service (and many outside it) of things that went wrong and analyse what was good and bad about the actions that people took in dealing with them. British Airways does the same with its own internal flight safety magazine and its own strong flight safety organisation, as do most other large airlines. If an airline pilot has a hiccup with a Boeing 757, the story is quickly with the Boeing Airplane Company and from there shortly afterwards into the hands of Boeing 757 pilots the world over. All manufacturers support their passenger-carrying aircraft in this way. But smaller aircraft are not forgotten. In Britain the Civil Aviation Authority publishes a safety information leaflet every few months, together with a detailed list of facts about incidents that have occurred to smaller general aviation aircraft, and circulates them to all operators and owners of light aircraft. Everybody learns from these stories. Without doubt their publication prevents many instances of history repeating itself by steering people away from courses of action that have caused tragedy elsewhere. Most pilots of light aircraft have flown themselves at one time or another into situations where they have suddenly realised "this has all the makings of being a very bad idea" or words to that effect, thankfully in enough time. That timely thought may have been the result of their initial training, long ago, but it is much more likely to have been the result of an incident they recently read about in the CAA leaflets or in 'Flight Safety', published by the General Aviation Safety Council.

But all these accident and incident reports, follow-up analyses in specialist magazines, 'road-show' presentations by the CAA, publicity campaigns about common hazards etc., effective though they are, all have one basic flaw. They all rely on things having gone wrong in the first place! What is worse, when things went wrong for the first time, you could almost invariably find someone who said, "I told you so!" So flight safety specialists began to ask themselves a more fundamental question: "What do we have to do to prevent things going wrong in the first place?" Some of the actions that resulted were very innovative. Not surprisingly, one of them involved listening to people early enough, and acting on what they said, to deny them the chance of ever being able to say, "I told you so!" Listening to people who CHIRP.

CHIRP is the UK's Confidential Human factors Incident Reporting Programme and it is now run from Farnborough as a registered charity. It is funded by a grant from the Civil Aviation Authority (CAA), which in turn receives its money from the air transport industry. CHIRP was set up jointly by the CAA and the RAF's Institute of Aviation Medicine (IAM) in 1982. A similar organisation had been set up in the USA following an accident when an airliner had flown into the ground after the published approach map to Washington's Dulles Airport had misled the crew. The investigation had revealed that a crew in another airline had previously been misled in a similar way and had spotted their error in time, but there had been no arrangements in place to ensure that mistakes of this kind could be reported confidentially, publicised quickly and action taken to solve them. At that time Britain already had a Mandatory Occurrence Reporting system for air incidents, but this system was principally for reporting when something had broken or when someone's mistake had been noticed by another agency. There weren't many near-occurrences of the true human factors kind, the *mea nearly culpa* variety, and the Chief Scientist at the CAA realised that the same sort of problem that had beset the American crews could also be encountered by British flight crews and go unreported. He and Air Commodore Tony Nicholson at the IAM resolved to pre-empt such a possibility with CHIRP. Intended at first for flight deck crew of public transport aircraft, CHIRP was soon extended to air traffic controllers after an inquiry into an air-miss incident revealed that human factors had been an issue, then to engineers and aircraft maintenance organisations. By 2001 it had been made available to aircraft designers and builders, to the operators of small aircraft, and then to those vital, but often overlooked, contributors to safe flying operations, the cabin crew.

As its name suggests, CHIRP concentrates on human factors. 'Human factors' is not, as a cynic might think, just a comfortable euphemism for mistakes; it also covers a host of other topics that include things such as misleading instrument displays and poor flight deck design (for example, switches that can be easily knocked when you go to operate something else). CHIRP concentrates on human factors because they are becoming the dominant ones in the causes of aviation accidents. This isn't because people are making more mistakes - the opposite is the case, people are making fewer mistakes in aviation than ever before. It is because the rate of accidents and incidents due to technical failures has been steadily reducing through the years. With new developments on the way this trend may continue, but it will take constant vigilance to ensure that it does. But the rate of contribution to accidents from human factors has remained remarkably constant and therefore these are increasingly dominant as one of the causes of accidents. Some wit recently expressed the opinion that aircraft of the future should be flown solely by the on-board systems, which should be monitored by a man with a dog. The man's job would be to feed the dog. The dog's job would be to bite the man if he touched anything. Definitely amusing, but even the serious thought behind the concept is unrealistic and a long way off. Only one system exists to make an airliner go around from a final approach to land when a vehicle strays on to the runway half a mile ahead, or to take other appropriate actions when one of a million other things pops up as a nasty surprise, which Murphy says it will. That system is the human brain and we are stuck with it for a few years yet. It is also the thing that designs and makes our aircraft systems so we really ought not to discard it too readily.

At first CHIRP attracted just a few reports every month. Initially aircrew found it difficult to believe that they could actually express their worries, for example about things like potentially dangerous nineteen-hour duty days (now long gone thank goodness, see Chapter 6), without their management finding out just who had done the complaining and marking their card. But it quickly became apparent that CHIRP was effective. The driving force behind its early days, the late Dr Roger Green at the IAM, delivered the goods and the word spread. Roger Green was a behavioural psychologist. He understood that people could occasionally do errant things and he understood the workings of the brain that caused them to do so. He also understood that aircrew were people and didn't stop being people just because they worked on a flight deck for a living. People make mistakes at work every day. When did you last make a mistake at work? Were you careless or deliberately negligent? Of course not. A situation built up around you that you misread perhaps, and with hindsight you made a mistake. Do you think that people in other occupations are somehow exempt from such things? Or that they should be? That would be another mistake.

Roger Green's favourite story concerned a man who went out into his back yard to fill a coal bucket. As he came back into the house he realised that he needed to go to the loo. The next thing he knew was that he was watching himself pour the coal from the bucket down the toilet. Are there equivalent mistakes to be made on an aircraft's flight deck, on the bridge of a ship, or in a railway signal box? Soon after CHIRP started, one co-pilot reported that on the approach he had asked the captain to lower the next stage of flap, only for the captain (who had acknowledged the request correctly) to lean across and shut down the fuel cock to the starboard engine… Murphy's Law again – if it can happen some day it will, so either design the system to prevent it happening or watch out for it and catch it. This one they caught, but losing one engine out of two on final approach must have set the pulses racing. Aviation people report to CHIRP the circumstances that led them into making, or trying to make, other errors. Those circumstances might have been combinations of shift patterns that caused them unusual tiredness, features of flight deck or instrument design that confused them, procedures that were unnecessarily difficult to carry out or just plain infuriating, communications that broke down. Aircrew also report how personal problems affect their flying performance, for example how being away from home at a crucial time, such as when children are sitting examinations, is becoming an issue because number one (or possibly number two or even three) wife is finding it all rather a pain. In recent years it has become much more common in British Airways for aircrew to elect a life-style change from long-range operations to short-haul and vice-versa, as it suits them. This was seldom, if ever, possible when British European Airways and the British Overseas Airways Corporation were two rival and very separate entities.

CHIRP is now an established element in air operations in Britain today. Following receipt of a report, the Director and staff at CHIRP will agree a course of action in consultation with the Reporter. Any follow-up action taken as a result is fed back to the Reporter. Reports received that have a wider bearing on aviation activities, or which present unusual or difficult issues, are referred to Advisory Boards set up for the purpose. These Boards, separately constituted for Air Transport, General Aviation and Cabin Crew, discuss issues and give guidance to the Director in their respective fields. The over-riding priority, however, is that the follow-up process will successfully and absolutely preserve the anonymity of the original reporter. The system works well and it is to the credit of CHIRP's current structure and way of working that it retains the confidence and respect of three very different interest groups: the users, the operational managements and the regulatory bodies. CHIRP in aviation has been so successful that, in 2003, a similar programme went operational with the UK's maritime industry.

For the most part CHIRP operates discreetly in putting things right. On one occasion, however, a CHIRP report led to some extensive publicity following the publication of a dis-identified version of the report in the CHIRP newsletter *Feedback*, in fact some time after the matter had been resolved. Neither the operator nor anyone connected with the report was named in the *Feedback* article, as is normal practice. However, the aviation press picked up the story and proceeded to conduct its own enquiries, leading to an assumption as to the airline concerned. The report concerned a foreign carrier and outside the CAA's immediate jurisdiction. When the safety of a foreign carrier in UK airspace is the issue, the matter becomes one for the Government. In this particular case the then Department of the Environment, Transport and the Regions (DETR) directed the CAA to enquire further into the matter.

The story illustrates beautifully the practical meaning of the principle of 'airmanship' described in Chapter 9: everyone, absolutely everyone involved with aircraft, whatever their role, has a duty to look out for danger and act when they see it. In this case the CHIRP reporter was a ground engineer who was curious as to why a four-engined long-haul aircraft had not parked at the stand to which it had been allocated, but at another stand much closer to the taxiway. Once on the flight deck he (she?) noticed that the electronic displays showed that two of the four fuel tanks were indicating empty and were displaying amber warning lights. The contents displayed in the other two tanks were also much lower than aircraft of this type usually showed before refuelling. The engineer knew that if that type of aircraft had to perform a go around from a landing approach, the standard procedure was to link each engine to a different tank. But two of the tanks were empty. He also queried if the total fuel remaining would be enough for the aircraft to divert to another airport. Asking around, he found that this was not the first time this airline's aircraft had arrived with this sort of fuel state, so he raised a CHIRP.

The subsequent investigation resulted in discussions with the carrier concerning the need to carry adequate fuel reserves when landing at a UK destination. The previous practice stopped and the publicity that the case generated sent a warning to other operators across the world that the professionalism of British aviation people was likely to defeat any ideas for potentially risky practices that they might be tempted with. Not when operating into Britain you don't! Britain is the place where people CHIRP.

While using the foresight and professional judgement of aviation people is one way to identify things that will bite you if you don't attend to them, another way is to stage a 'mock accident'. Back in the late 1950s, RAF flight safety staffs noticed that accidents rarely had one cause. Usually a combination of circumstances came together and added up to a disaster. If any one of the circumstances had been missing, the accident would probably have been averted. The same logic was apparent in incidents that were almost accidents. Where a crew had had a near miss it was often clear that, if one other factor had not acted that day in their favour, a total accident would have happened. Too many of the factors that made up accidents were entirely preventable. Many were due to local procedures or management. It would clearly be a good idea to identify those that were set to bite you before a full Board of Inquiry did it for you! With only a little lateral thought, the notion of the 'mock accident' was born.

The principle is simple. You don't have to lose aircraft and people to learn the lessons of an accident. You just *pretend* you have had an accident, then go through the usual steps to find all the lessons! An expensive process? Yes, but try having a real accident, it dents the cheque book rather more. Typically the flight safety staff on an RAF station will select a squadron, perhaps an individual aircraft or crew, certainly a type of sortie. One day as the aircraft and crew taxies into its dispersal after a successful trip the flight safety people will descend on it as if it had not returned, impound the aircraft with all its data recording systems, lock away all the operations paperwork, aircrew training records and engineering documentation, impound the air traffic control tapes, etc. They will then set up the mechanism of a full board of inquiry on the assumption that the aircraft has been lost in a particular circumstance – crashed into a hillside, caught fire at 20,000 feet, whatever. They will then examine the evidence painstakingly for clues as to why this should have happened. Even with the aircraft safely in its hangar, there will be plenty. All the ugly truths that would have emerged, had the accident been a real one, will also emerge from this analysis. Why was the pilot out of low-level practice? Why was the flight authorised when the visibility was poor? Was the met forecast correct? Was the fact that the ejection seats were due servicing, but had been granted an extension, a factor in the crew's inability to escape? Why had the aircraft been 'carrying' a snag in the navigation/attack system for the past three weeks? Where is the documentation certifying the six-monthly safety checks on another system that were due three months ago and which everybody is sure were done?

As the average reader goes through this list, his or her blood is understandably likely to run a little cold. But that coldness is nothing, absolutely nothing, compared with the chill in the kidneys that a squadron executive will experience if he or she ever sits for real in the hot seat of a Board of Inquiry into the deaths of a couple of close friends and the loss of a valuable aircraft, and hears that type of question emerging from the investigation. The tightening of procedures, management practices, technical standards and a dozen other things can all be achieved without having a real accident. Just have a mock one! Aviation people wonder why more managers of other complex systems such as the railways don't also use the concept; the nuclear industry certainly does.

18

A Watch on the Skies

Every day a great deal happens behind the scenes to make sure that flying for everybody, but especially airline passengers, is as routine and as safe as possible. While a book of this size cannot possibly do justice to everybody involved, there are nevertheless two groups of people who must be included if this book is to be complete. The first is the air traffic controllers. Without the men and women in earphones looking at the radar screens and out of their control tower windows, very little would run safely or smoothly in the air transport business.

British skies are very crowded, more so than those of most nations across the world because in and over Britain there is a lot of economic activity taking place within a very small area of land. One USAF transport pilot, used to the huge clear skies over California and Nevada but who found himself based in Europe, just loves the cloudy British weather. This is because, flying in the UK on a clear day, he sees so many other aircraft out of his flight deck window that he ends up flying with his elbows tucked in, to miss them all. "You could get out and walk on them, some days", he complains. So British clouds he loves. "Flying in cloud, you have nothing to worry about!" he says, confident that the other aircraft couldn't possibly still be there. But they are - British and foreign, civil and military, and lots of them. Keeping them safely apart is a challenging task.

Air traffic controllers are a self-effacing lot. I challenge you to name me a famous air traffic controller. Of course you can't. But even when you ask that question in the air traffic control community itself, you get a similar response. In the last fifty years, air traffickers would have you believe that nobody in particular within their profession has had a single good idea. Rather, all the thousands of good ideas that make up the robust and safe air traffic control system that aviators and their passengers enjoy today came, not from anybody in particular, but from 'the team'. In air traffic control 'the team' is all, and even the bright lights that led the organisation when major decisions were made will not claim any credit for the benefits that have flowed from those decisions. "Well," said one, "I don't know who thought of it first. It was a sort of team idea and we all signed up to it."

Like most of the aviation industry, air traffic control over the years has spent a great deal of its time trying to spot problems before they arose and doing something about them before they bit. A typical example was the initiative that led to the formation of the National Air Traffic Control Services in 1962. In the late 1950s there had been some concern about the increasing number of 'air-misses' between civil and military aircraft. If that sounds too comforting, calling them 'near-collisions' focuses the mind rather better. At that time there was little coordination between the civil and military ATC authorities, and both public and politicians were becoming aware of the fact, as well as the aircraft operators and air traffic controllers themselves.

So over forty years ago, after a few scares, a small national ATC planning group was formed to study what would be needed to form a joint civil and military ATC system for Britain in the late 1960s and 1970s. It recommended a unified organisation, jointly run and jointly staffed by both military and civil air traffic controllers. Crucially, it saw the need for a single organisation to decide and then implement national policies for air traffic control. After the usual consideration by ministers and their staffs, the report was accepted and National Air Traffic Control Services, as it was then called, was formed in 1962. (Only nine years later did it become NATS, National Air Traffic Services. The cynics said they had lost Control!) The first Controller was a retired RAF air vice-marshal, therefore half-military and half-civilian, but the succession plan called for the post of Controller to alternate between a serving RAF officer and a civilian.

Soon after the new organisation was formed, it became very clear to some at the working level that the detailed plans for a new London Air Traffic Control Centre were flawed. The fundamental problem with manual air traffic control stems from the fact that, as the volume of traffic grows, the immediately logical solution is to split the airspace up into smaller and smaller sectors so that one controller can handle the load safely. The trouble is that this brings with it the need to hand over from sector to sector. Soon the handing-over and coordination can become as big a task as the actual controlling and therefore something of a distraction. To some of the senior London staff, the plans for the new London centre did little to solve these and other very evident problems, and in some cases threatened to make matters worse. Egged on by his colleagues, Bill Woodruff said as much to the Controller and he got the quickest and most positive response possible. "If you and your lot don't like the plans, then get on and provide new ones". Bill was given an office, a secretary (whose early vital role was to come up with coffee or tea every hour, on the hour) and six air traffic control officers with current operational experience at the busy Southern Centre, three full-time and three part-time. They were Geoff Large, 'Lucky' Craven, and Reg Simmonds, with John Toseland, Tony Albertini and 'Barney' Hughs part-time. At the end of December 1964 they were given just three months to complete their tasks, starting with re-planning the airways sectors with the new philosophy (learned from visits to USA ATC centres) of designing sector 'suites' where everybody involved with a sector was co-located and in touch with what everybody else was doing. They also had to redesign the operations room in detail and specify exactly what the radar displays should show and what communications would be needed between the various elements. Last, they had to test their solution with the telecoms specialists to make sure that they had not designed the technically impossible.

Bill Woodruff and the six went back to their jobs in late March 1965 feeling much more than two-and-a-half months older. Six years later, on the last day of January 1971, the new London Air Traffic Control Centre (LATCC) came into being at West Drayton. To the seven people who had been involved at the very beginning, the Operations Room bore a comforting resemblance to those plans made in such haste six years before. What changes there were had largely been made to take advantage of new radar and telecommunications technologies that had become available during the intervening years.

In the nearly forty years since the original design, the philosophy that Bill Woodruff and his team of six put down on their blank sheets of paper has stood the test of time. Since the 1970s air traffic has grown by an average of five percent every year, and in some individual prosperous years has jumped by over seven percent. London's Airports now handle much more traffic than was ever envisioned by LATCC's original design. Growth in air traffic has made it necessary to create new air traffic control centres with greater capacity. New radar and computing technologies have made this possible with electronic 'hand-overs' of aircraft replacing verbal ones, enabling airspace to be divided up into even smaller chunks. At West Drayton, Terminal Control now handles all aircraft over Southern England at the lower altitudes. At Swanwick in Hampshire, the En-Route Centre handles the high-level traffic above those altitudes, much of it crossing through UK airspace from one country to another. Each day over 5,000 commercial aircraft fly through UK airspace and within ten years this figure is conservatively estimated to rise to 7,000 and possibly 9,500 flights. But at Swanwick and the other centres that replace LATCC, the principles and building blocks from the 1960s still form the basis of the new ways of working. All controllers working a sector now assuredly have the same radar picture and their information is electronic, enabling each to be sure of exactly what the other controller is doing without having to be co-located or in voice contact any more. NATS continues to be managed and manned jointly by civilian and military controllers. One consequence is that, as a military pilot flying along a civil airway towards your military destination, your hand-over between controllers feels so seamless that you quickly lose track of whether the controller handling you is a military or a civil one. What you can tell, however, especially if you fly into British airspace after a long journey overseas, is just how good they all are. This is not a recent accomplishment; the USAF transport pilot in his C-130 Hercules was frankly astonished when he first flew into Britain from Germany back in the 1970s.

"I was going to Upper Heyford. I had flight-planned using airways to Honiley, near Birmingham, where I planned to descend out of controlled airspace, turn back south-east, contact Upper Heyford radar and get them to give me some vectors. I never stood a chance with a plan that complicated. The airways controller was a girl who sounded as if she was about sixteen. Halfway to Birmingham from London as we were bumbling along at about twelve thousand feet, she tells me to commence a maximum rate descent and turn left forty degrees. It was a bit of a surprise, but being a new guest in your splendid country, and a gentleman, of course I did as I was told. Then she tells me to level at eight thousand feet, turn left again on to a heading of 070 degrees, and tune to the Upper Heyford ILS (instrument landing system). I did that and as I rolled out on the heading, in the thickest darkest cloud I had ever been in, the ILS needles went 'zap!' into a perfect cross, bang on the centrelines of the Upper Heyford localiser and the glide-path!" He paused for breath. "This kid," he went on, "not only had the geometry in her head to position me from altitude in the airway into the Heyford approach, she even knew what my aircraft was capable of, in a max rate descent, to get me there! It saved us at least twenty minutes flying time and I was very, very impressed. You do realise, don't you, that you will never, ever, get an air traffic control service like that anywhere else in the world? I *love* flying in your country!"

If other people's air traffic control may not seem to be quite as good on occasion, some would say it is not as fair sometimes, either. At the old Munich Riem airport in the 1980s a certain rivalry developed between British Airways and Lufthansa, both of which had services departing at 8 a.m. for London. They were business people's specials, and business people are in a hurry. The game was simple: load your passengers as quickly as possible, push back from the gate ahead of your rival, and whoever is first down to the runway is first to take off and hence first to London. On the days when you win this competition, you can point out to your thoroughly satisfied customers how better off they are flying British Airways/Lufthansa (delete as appropriate) because, if they would be so kind as to look out of their starboard windows they would see the opposition's eight o'clock service to London languishing at the hold. You are going to get them to London first, all part of the service, and flying that (or any other) morning by Lufthansa/British Airways (delete again as appropriate) would just have been a huge mistake, wouldn't it?

This game went on for some time and one morning it was the British Airways aircraft that managed to be first away and first down to the runway. When it got there, however, Munich ATC ordered it to pull over into the hold area, whereupon they allowed the Lufthansa aircraft behind to overtake it and line up on the runway first. In vain the BA pilot protested to a silent Munich ATC. As he complained again, demanding an explanation for the injustice, the Lufthansa Boeing 737 to London was lifting off the runway and tucking its wheels up. Still no reply from air traffic control, but the airborne German pilot pressed his transmit button and kindly offered the reason. "Ach so!" he said, "it is because I left my towel on ze runway last night."

Cheating works both ways, however. For years European airline pilots, including those of Lufthansa, could not understand why aircraft of the small British airline Dan-Air seemed to keep receiving direct routings across Europe from the big air traffic control centre at Maastricht when everybody else invariably had their requests refused and were told to go the long way round, from beacon to beacon. They had no way of knowing that Dan-Air's splendid management had arranged for a couple of crates of very good beer to be sent to the Maastricht controllers' social club every Friday night. Over the years, that typical people-gesture by Dan-Air's bosses saved the airline millions of pounds in fuel bills, but alas even that was not enough to save Dan-Air from eventual financial embarrassment and take-over by British Airways. Dan-Air crews were a spirited bunch, however, and the few who were re-employed by British Airways discovered one final futile gesture of independence in the first few weeks after the take-over. They found that the huge 'British Airways' logos, newly stuck on to their aircraft at considerable expense to obliterate their beloved Dan-Air livery, were peculiarly vulnerable if flown through rain clouds at 300 knots. Air traffic controllers must have been a bit puzzled for a while at pilots' requests for course changes that seemed to take aircraft towards cloud build-ups, rather than away from them, but chasing rain clouds became a good game for a couple of weeks. The seabed of the English Channel must be littered with huge curled-up pieces of plastic with the fading words 'British Airways' writ large upon them.

If air traffic controllers are one silent, but vital, force behind safe flying, aviation weather forecasters, or 'met men', are definitely another. You could say, however, that while air traffic controllers make flying possible, the met men usually make it inadvisable! Safe aircraft operations depend on accurate weather forecasting, and aviation meteorology has evolved with a detail and precision all its own. It was not always so; the late Jimmy Edwards, the comedian, used to tell a story against met men from his days as a Dakota (Douglas C-47 or DC-3) pilot during the War. One of his colleagues, taxying round the perimeter track of his base airfield in low cloud and blinding rain, was just about to pass the control tower when he heard on the radio the local met forecaster delivering his 'actual' report for the airfield. Apparently it was a beautiful sunny day there! Incensed, the pilot stopped his Dakota right outside the control tower, engines running, set the parking brakes and jumped out of the aircraft via the door at the back. In what was possibly the first ever recorded instance of perimeter-track rage, he rushed into the tower and into the basement to find the hapless met man. He grabbed him by the scruff of the neck and dragged him up the stairs and into the daylight, or what little there was of it.

"What's *that*?" he yelled, pointing at the deluge. The rain ran down the met man's hair into his collar.

"It's not on my chart" the poor met man replied.

Things have much improved since then, but it is difficult for the layman in the street to appreciate how much. This is because the weather forecasts that we get, as the public, are necessarily general and are designed for a wide area. The weather forecast for a specific point, such as an airfield, can be made much more accurate and detailed. Take today, as these words are being written, in the county of Surrey about twelve miles south-west of London Heathrow Airport. The public forecast on the radio for the whole south-east of England, accurate enough for social, domestic and pleasure purposes, has been for a cloudy day with occasional spells of rain. What that leaves out, of course, is the 'how much' and the 'when'. Compare this with the forecast for nearby Heathrow, on the strength of which pilots getting their met briefing at their departure airfields will decide whether or not to take off for London and how much diversion fuel to carry. Translating the various codes in which the forecast is transmitted to the world's airports, the forecast for London Heathrow for the next nine hours reads:

"In general, the wind direction at the surface will be from 150 degrees and its strength will be 6 knots. Visibility will be more than 10 kilometres, the cloud nearest the surface will be broken ('broken' is defined as covering 5 to 7 eighths of the sky) and will have a base of 4,000 feet. Temporarily, between 1400 and 1900 hours local, visibility will go down to 6,000 metres in showers of rain, when there will be broken cloud at 1,400 feet and more broken cloud with a base of 2,500 feet. This latter cloud will be cumulo-nimbus, heavy shower cloud carrying a risk of lightning and thunder. Between 1700 and 1900 hours local, the wind velocity will change to 210 degrees and 10 knots, and between 2200 and 2300 hours tonight the cloud will remain broken but will have a base of 1,000 feet."

"Better to be down here wishing you were up there,
than up there wishing you were down here!"

As well as publishing hourly reports of actual meteorological conditions (METARs) and terminal area forecasts (TAFs), the forecasters at an airfield such as Heathrow are available for face-to-face consultation if someone is planning to fly somewhere unusual. On the larger RAF stations it is the same, with the morning 'met brief' in operations from the met man being something of a focal point; all the aircrew and station executives are there, all in the same place at the same time, just once in the day. Station met briefs can be demanding experiences for junior forecasters, nurtured as they are in teams, in the warmth of large buildings in Bracknell, Exeter or wherever. On an RAF station they have to perform solo and they have to get used to the demands of a Group Captain who holds them personally responsible for the weather and who wants to know exactly when this foul stuff is going to go away so that his flying programme can be planned, weapons ranges booked and air-to-air refuelling tankers tasked, etc. One older, rather droll, met man on one RAF station, knowing the usual mood of his audience on a very wet morning, decided to pre-empt the question.

"This rain is from an active cold front passing over us. It will clear here at 1112 hours this morning."

A gale of laughter ran around the operations briefing room and a couple of pilots set the chimers on their watches as a reminder. At 1100 that morning the pilots met, soaking wet, in the crew-room of one of the squadrons to drink a coffee, to admire the rain (still stair-rodding it down outside), and to indulge in a traditional whinge about the inadequacies of GroundPounders in general and met men in particular. At 1110 hours, in mid-rant, they were a bit surprised when the rain suddenly stopped. At 1112 hours they were absolutely astonished when the cloud lifted and the sun came out.

19

Wings to Come

If, after all this, you finally believe in the Wright Brothers (and I really hope that you do), you must be stunned by the progress that aviation has made over the past hundred years and may possibly be wondering "what comes next?" December 2003 marked the start of the second centennial of powered flight. For the ordinary man and woman who needs to fly on business or to go on holiday, it seems to be a good start from a position of some strength. We have a world-wide air transport industry with a large capacity, offering safe and affordable flying to millions of people using some of the cleverest technologies in everyday use. Incredibly, routine supersonic air travel is no more because it both came and went in the first hundred years. There are no plans to replace the Concorde and there won't be until the environmental penalties of supersonic flight are solved and its economics become sensible too. That will take some time, by which I mean several decades. We now look forward, it seems, to years of 'more of the same', where 'the same' is safe and comfortable subsonic flight in large aircraft. Is there really anything else left to achieve in aviation?

There is much left to achieve. There seem to be as many problems as ever for future aviation people to sink their teeth into and solve; some will have been apparent from this book. But speed of air travel is no longer the driving problem that it once was. In the USA, NASA abandoned its research programmes into high speed flight in 1999. What is the point of spending billions to make a new type of aircraft that flies fifty, even one hundred mph faster when it will arrive at a destination like London only to 'hold' in the Ockham stack for thirty minutes before being allowed to land at a congested airport like Heathrow? A Heathrow where the queues for immigration will delay the passenger by as much again? There are more important problems to solve in air transport than speed through the air because the choke points in air travel are now clearly elsewhere in the system. Air traffic control is under continuous pressure to improve its performance and runway capacity is a major limiting factor. For the aircraft itself, the three current types of problem that top the list are those involving safety, the environment and operating economics. But these are always accompanied by another challenge: if those problems are going to be solved, the quality and effectiveness of aviation's people must be maintained.

Current levels of safety and environmental pollution from air transport may (just) be acceptable to the majority of the public, but that is very unlikely to remain the case. Leave things as they are and, in thirty years time, the air transport industry could appear much like the British railway industry does now. First (and it always should be first), take safety. Current levels of global safety are such that, on average, between twenty and thirty fatal accidents occur to public transport aircraft every year. Of those, half happen to regional or commuter aircraft, half to airliners flying longer distances, and the total number of fatalities involved is just over one thousand. The current lack of popular concern about such an annual record, coupled with the rising demand for air travel, signals that this is a 'socially acceptable' accident rate, although aviation people will be quick to protest that of course there can be no such thing above a figure of zero. But will such an accident rate stay generally 'socially acceptable'? Consider the forecasts for global growth in air transport in the next thirty years. By 2030 the number of flights is forecast to treble. The current accident rate, if maintained, would result in a fatal air accident somewhere in the world every four days. The world might be lucky and get a whole fortnight with none, then four would occur two days running. Air accidents make strong images and powerful TV news: flames, smoke, wreckage, tragic shots of personal effects, mystery, demands for quick answers, grief from next of kin. It doesn't matter how good the overall statistics are. Even if they show an improving trend on historic levels, the accident that happened yesterday is there for everyone to see in their living room. Faced with often-repeated images of that nature, how long would the public continue to perceive that air transport was safe? If that perception ever started to crumble, it would be by then too late to reverse that trend with any quick or simple measures. Accident rates do not respond to such things. Decades of work would be needed to restore air transport's record and reputation, during which time even more damage would inevitably be done. The British rail industry, which has suffered some dramatic troubles in recent years, constitutes an awful warning to all those connected with the air transport industry who might be tempted to rest on illusory laurels and sacrifice the next decade's safety investments for next year's profit figure. Aviation people will need to strive as hard as ever if they are to steer their profession away from the fate of the British rail network.

They will need to tackle current safety issues with the same determination and relentlessness that has characterised the efforts of their predecessors over the past hundred years. There will never be a shortage of such issues; experience shows that as aviation people solve one problem, another raises its head for urgent attention. One of the current common causes of contemporary accidents to large passenger-carrying aircraft is 'CFIT' – Controlled Flight Into Terrain. Invariably there are many factors, technical and human, that contribute to any one accident, but the outcome of a CFIT accident involves a crew, usually at night or in cloud, very confidently and calmly flying their aircraft into solid ground that they didn't know about. Fortunately, new systems are now being fitted that are designed to defeat that possibility, and these make use of the networks of satellite navigation systems, the American Global Positioning System (GPS) or the proposed new European Galileo system. These systems are numbers of satellites broadcasting simultaneous signals that a simple receiver in an aircraft can interpret into a three-dimensional 'fix' over the earth, accurate to within a few metres. Three-dimensions means an accurate position and height. With that information compared with a stored computer-memory model of the earth's surface that is also three-dimensional (a 'global terrain database') and some clever real-time computing in the aircraft, the aircraft's Terrain Awareness Warning System will warn a crew when the velocity vector of their aircraft is taking them towards something solid, anywhere in the world and at any height. More than that, it will indicate the flight path that they must take, the 'curly tube in the sky', to fly out of trouble. For aircraft approaching poorly equipped airports in mountainous terrain, the new equipment promises to confer the same boost to future safety that the automatic landing system did for aircraft needing to land at European airports on foggy nights in the 1970s.

Other new technologies will come too, but they will have to be either safety-related or have an overwhelming economic benefit. They are unlikely any more to arrive in the shape of 'new technology for new technology's sake'. Innovations now, in aviation as in many other strands of life, have to pass a very stern economic test so that the value of their benefits will exceed their cost. Currently planned developments in the design of passenger-carrying airliners seem to promise a saving of about twenty percent in fuel consumption compared with today's machines. Of that, only about a third will come from improvements to the efficiency of engines. Slightly more than another third will come from better aerodynamics of the aircraft, and much of this will come from micro-electromechanical systems that sense and control airflow. For example, vortex generators (Chapter 10) in the future will not be fixed to the wing where they can cause drag throughout the flight – they will simply pop up when the control surface behind them actually needs them. Finally, new materials and more efficient lighter structures will contribute to the rest of the improvement in fuel consumption.

Until now, aircraft have achieved their stability from their shape, with tailplanes contributing a stabilising down-force (Chapter 3). That is no longer necessary – the controls themselves can be operated by 'fly-by-wire' artificial stability systems to do that job instead. Systems like this have been providing part of the aircraft's stability, with complete reliability, for some years. Making use of such reliable systems to do the whole job of providing an aircraft's stability means a smaller (or even no) tailplane, which means less weight. Further, a smaller down-force at the back of the aircraft means that less lift is needed from the wing, and both of these factors will reduce the overall drag and give efficiency benefits for the operation of the aircraft.

The rate of fuel burn is a big issue, not just from the obvious aspect of operating cost, but also from the point of view of the environment. Oxides of nitrogen apart, aircraft at altitude produce trails of condensed water vapour ('contrails') that have long been suspected of contributing to a 'greenhouse' effect and warming the earth's surface. The aftermath of the September 11th terrorist attacks in the USA in 2001 provided a unique proof that this is so. All commercial flights were grounded at that time for a few days and meteorologists discovered that the lack of contrails in the sky contributed to measurably different temperatures on the ground below, higher by day (no contrail cloud blocking the sun) and lower by night (no cloud 'tea-cosy' effect). As a result, aircraft may soon find themselves routed away from areas where contrails could cause local environmental damage, or be assigned to different altitudes where contrails will not form. As either measure will increase the cost of air transport, an engineering solution built into the aircraft would be better. Until the 2001 discovery about the effect of contrails, people had talked confidently that hydrogen would become the aircraft fuel of choice to replace kerosene. But hydrogen-burning engines would produce more

water vapour, and therefore more contrails, than kerosene-burners. Hydrogen may not be the answer when part of the pollution effect from aircraft is clearly one of greenhouse temperature change.

For fuel burn savings greater than the twenty percent currently foreseen, radical changes to the shapes that we see in the sky, and that we currently associate with air transport, are likely. Forget wings and fuselages; the future shape is likely to be a blended wing-body, or BWB, the whole shape containing fuel, passengers and cargo. Control surfaces will be a thing of the past, because the aircraft will develop the forces to manoeuvre by flexing its overall shape, the flexible composite materials used in its structure enabling it to do that. There will be few passenger windows, if any, but doubtless passengers will have the electronic equivalent of several windows on their personal video screens in front of them. Engines are likely to be on pylons on top of the wing so that any noise from their intakes, bodies or exhausts is shielded from critical observers on the ground. Therefore with such a design, the airframe itself passing through the air is likely to be the biggest source of noise. The early noise work on the gliding VC-10 at RAE Bedford in 1974 (Chapter 13) is likely to be the starting point of much new research that will be needed in that area to ensure that a BWB aircraft can travel almost silently over the suburbs on its way to a night landing at the world's biggest airports. But, whatever new shapes and philosophies make it into the sky, the first, second and last issues will always be safety, safety, and safety. Aviation's people will see to that.

What about aviation's people in the future, in particular the newcomers? The education, training and experience they will receive will make a vital contribution to their performance in the aviation profession. Education in schools has been changing rapidly and noticeably in recent years and for the aviation industry some of the changes may be a cause for concern, particularly the general levels of achievement in maths and physics. Can the post-education training of pilots, engineers and other aviation professionals fill the important gaps by imparting the necessary skills of, say, mental arithmetic, when their schooling has not? Are those skills, vital in aviation during the past hundred years, actually going to be necessary with future aircraft and systems? Murphy says they will be, because things can still go wrong. What about other old-fashioned things, such as manual flying skills? Twenty years ago, most airline pilots had thousands of hours of manual flying experience. They had flown military aircraft if they were ex-Service, or they had been on the fleets of the early civil aircraft types that demanded long periods of hands-on flying, or they had spent some time instructing in flying schools before their first airline job. Then, when faced with astonishing circumstances such as failure of two engines out of two over the Atlantic many miles from the Azores (in 2001) or high over Canada (in 1983), pilots with these backgrounds had the skills to glide their stricken aircraft to safe landings at unplanned airfields. Will airline pilots of the future, trained to be line pilots on safe (hence, easy-to-fly) aircraft, be able to do the same if that particular Murphy comes their way? If it does, it may well be many years since they last did a glide approach for real during their initial training in light aircraft. Many current airline pilots recognise this as an issue and fly gliders or light aircraft at their own expense to ensure that they maintain their total flying expertise. Pilots on intercontinental routes get fewer landings and less 'hands-on' time per flying hour than their colleagues on short-haul, and opportunities for reinforcement of those basic skills can be a bit 'thin in the air' (so to speak) in a pilot's everyday flying. When Murphy strikes, he can strike big. On the afternoon of 1 November 1997 a huge Airbus 340 of Virgin Atlantic Airways approached London Heathrow from Los Angeles and, eight miles out with the gear selected, one main undercarriage leg refused to come down. Only two passengers were slightly injured and all were full of praise when Captain Tim Barnby, all other options exhausted, made an exemplary emergency landing and succeeded in coming to a stop on the runway centreline, the key to minimal damage in such a situation. But this pilot's flying skills were top-notch; he was also the current British Aerobatics champion.

Some of Captain Barnby's passengers may subsequently have been surprised to discover this, but they should not have been. It is so easy to assume that the little bi-plane that you see performing aerobatics over the Oxfordshire countryside on a Sunday afternoon is some rich kid from the City, enjoying himself noisily at the expense of others. It is much more likely to be someone who will be in the front left-hand seat of the aircraft taking you to Frankfurt tomorrow morning. One day a few hundred people, on their way to somewhere similar or coming back home to London at a time when Murphy decides to put in an appearance, may be very grateful for that pilot's exceptional flying skills and the dedication that caused him or her to keep them ever sharp.

All this means that aviation people, and especially young people who want a career in aviation, have as many personal challenges as ever and lots to look forward to. Those three big issues: ever-improving aviation safety, lower and lower environmental impact from aircraft operations, and steadily improving operating economics, will be enough to keep the finest and most enthusiastic minds busy in the years ahead. The history of the past hundred years tells us, however, that the owners of those minds will only succeed if they are allowed to work in the same manner as the people who have made aviation such a success before them. They must be free to learn from their mistakes, and free to share the lessons from them. If that can be achieved, the spirit, attitude and achievement of flying people will stay much as they always have been - upbeat, open, and successful. Those who are privileged to work in aviation will enjoy that same special working life as their predecessors, a career with an inspiring secret element that seems sadly to be fast disappearing from many other professions. I do hope that element has become apparent from the stories and characters in these pages: working with flying people is *fun*.

Abbreviations

AAIB	Air Accidents Investigation Branch (UK)
ABS	Anti-lock Braking System
AEF	Air Experience Flight
APU	Auxiliary power unit
ARB	Air Registration Board (UK)
ARL	Aeronautical Research Laboratory (Australia)
ATC	Air Training Corps
ATC	Air Traffic Control
ATGB	Air Turbine Gear Box
AVPIN	Aviation Specification Iso-Propyl Nitrate (a monofuel)
AVTUR	Aviation Turbine Fuel
BA	British Airways
BAC	British Aircraft Corporation
BAe	British Aerospace
BBC	British Broadcasting Corporation
BEA	British European Airways
BLEU	Blind Landing Experimental Unit
BOAC	British Overseas Airways Corporation
BWB	Blended Wing-Body
CAA	Civil Aviation Authority (UK)
CAADRP	Civil Aircraft Airworthiness Data Recording Programme
CCF	Combined Cadet Force
CCWR	Cloud and Collision Warning Radar
CFIT	Controlled Flight Into Terrain
CHAG	Chain Arrester Gear
CHIRP	Confidential Human factors Incident Reporting Programme (UK)
C-in-C	Commander-in-Chief
CISTR	Glider checks: Controls, Instruments, Spoilers, Trim and Release
CVR	Cockpit Voice Recorder
DETR	Department of the Environment, Transport and the Regions (UK)
DNA	Deoxyribonucleic Acid
FAA	Federal Aviation Administration (USA)
FDR	Flight Data Recorder
FOD	Foreign Object Damage
GCE	General Certificate of Education
GPS	Global Positioning System
GPWS	Ground Proximity Warning System
HASELL	Checks preceding aerobatics – Height, Airframe, Security, Engine, Location, Lookout.
HF	High Frequency
HP	High pressure
IAM	Institute of Aviation Medicine
ILS	Instrument Landing System
JP3	Jet Provost Mark 3 trainer aircraft

KLM	KLM Royal Dutch Airlines (Koninklijke Luchtvaart Maatschappij)
LATCC	London Air Traffic Control Centre
METAR	Meteorological Actual Report of weather conditions at a location
MoD	Ministry of Defence (UK)
NASA	National Aeronautics and Space Administration (USA)
NATO	North Atlantic Treaty Organisation
NATS	National Air Traffic Services (UK)
NHS	National Health Service (UK)
NTSB	National Transportation Safety Board (USA)
QFE	Atmospheric pressure at aerodrome elevation or at runway threshold
RAAF	Royal Australian Air Force
RAE	Royal Aircraft Establishment
RAF	Royal Air Force
RHAG	Rotary Hydraulic Arrester Gear
RPM	Revolutions per minute
RVR	Runway Visual Range
STC	Standard Telecommunications and Cables
TAF	Terminal Area Forecast
UAS	University Air Squadron
USAF	United States Air Force
VHF	Very High Frequency
VIP	Very Important Person

UK Weights and Measures

As most of the circumstances described in this book pre-date the decimalisation of British currency and the metrication of many UK weights and measurements, some of the early terms have necessarily been used. Familiar to those over a certain age (and still preferred by some), they will nonetheless be archaic to other readers. For those readers who did not have to struggle at school with inches, feet, yards, ounces and pounds (let alone chains and furlongs), the following guide might prove useful:

1 foot (12 inches) equals 0.3048 metres
1 yard (3 feet) equals 0.9144 metres
1 mile (1,760 yards or 5,280 feet) equals 1.609 kilometres
1 nautical mile is 6,080 feet, being 1 minute (a sixtieth of a degree) of latitude
1 knot is 1 nautical mile per hour and equals 1.1515 mph
1 ounce equals 28.35 grammes
1 pound (lb) (16 ounces) equals 0.4536 kilogrammes
1 gallon (8 pints) equals 4.5455 litres
1 shilling (12 old pennies) equals 5 pence
20 shillings (i.e. 240 old pennies or 100 pence) equals £1
1 old penny equals 0.4167 pence

If you have enjoyed reading *Flying People* by Graham Perry
why not read its companion volume -

Whatever were you thinking of, Captain?
A Handbook for Airline Passengers

by

Captain John L. Morton

Morton is a retired pilot whose career ranged from flying mini-airliners that landed on the beach airfield of the Isle of Barra, to being a Training Captain on British Airways' wide-bodied aircraft. He describes this handy volume as guiding 'the interested layman' through the various aspects of a journey by air.

While this book describes some of the technical aspects of an air journey, jargon is minimised and the practical aspect of the content is lightened with anecdote and humour. Its ultimate objective is intended to suggest a relaxed and confident atmosphere to flying.

Whatever were you thinking of, Captain? is also illustrated by the artistic pen of *figment*, the nom-de-plume of John Reed, who is a long-time flight deck colleague of Morton.

Hailed as "...a mini-masterpiece" by the journal of the British Air Line Pilots Association, *The Log*.

Whatever were you thinking of, Captain?
by *Captain John L. Morton*
kea publishing
80 pages, 20 drawings, 4 maps and diagrams
Softback. Cover price £8.95. ISBN 0 9518958 5 0

Available from:
Kea Publishing, 14 Flures Crescent, Erskine, Renfrewshire PA8 7DJ, Scotland.
Please add 10% for postage and packing; 25% for air mail outside Europe.

Index